D1615967

NEW + NOTABLE PRODUCT DESIGN II

First published in the United States of America by:
Rockport Publishers, Inc.
146 Granite Street
Rockport, Massachusetts 01966-1299
Telephone: (508) 546-9590
Fax: (508) 546-7141

Distributed to the book trade in the United States by:
Consortium Book Sales and Distribution
1045 Westgate Drive
Saint Paul, MN 55114-0165

ISBN 1-56496-120-6

10 9 8 7 6 5 4 3 2 1

Art Director: Laura P. Herrmann
Designer: Stolze Design

Cover Photographs:
    (Front from top)
    1. Andrea Branzi, Michele De
    Lucchi, and Ettore Sottsass
    2. Pg. 100
    3. Pg. 169
    (Back from top)
    1. Pg. 179
    2. Pg. 166
    3. Pg. 173

Communications Consultant: Janet Blaich

Manufactured in Singapore by Regent
Publishing Services (S) Pte. Ltd.

NEW +

NOTABLE

PRODUCT

DESIGN II

ROCKPORT
PUBLISHERS

Rockport Publishers
Rockport, Massachusetts

Top Row
A. Robert Blaich with Herman Miller Inc. Designers circa 1975. Top: Charles Eames, D.J. DePree (chairman Emeritus), Robert Blaich, Robert Propst. Bottom: Ray Eames, George Nelson, Alexander Girard.
B. "Moving Sound", youth audio products
C. Videophone
D. Phillips "Collection", television

Second Row:
E. "Matchline", home entertainment system
F. "Cafe Gourmet", coffee maker
G. "Discoverer", youth television
H. "Integris–C", X-ray, diagnostic system

Third Row:
I. "Platinum", ultrasound imager
J. Dr. Robert Blaich, in the "Evoluon" Phillips Competence Center
K. "Ambiente" Exhibit, Berlin home of the future
L. Philishave "Rota", electric rotary shaver

Fourth Row:
M. Contemporary clock
N. "Collection", CD player & FM headphones
O. "CAFEtherm", coffee maker and carafe
P. "DIMlight", halogen lamps

Fifth Row:
Q. "Pro", track lighting system
R. Domestic appliances packaging
S. "PEOS", electronic office system
T. "Product Design and Corporate Strategy". Robert and Janet Blaich

The products shown were designed under Dr. Robert Blaich's direction as Senior Director of Philips Corporate Design, between 1980 and 1992.

TABLE of CONTENTS

Twenty years ago, designer and author George Nelson wrote in Fortune magazine:

"the industrial designer is an artist
because he shapes things in an effort
to give order and beauty to a mass of material,
and in so doing, he infuses an emotional content
into an inanimate article."

In the years since that idealistic definition of product designers, the majority of products rolling off production lines and into the hands of consumers were either bland, "black boxes" designed to mask complex interior technology, or arrogant proclaimers of high-tech design, bristling with buttons and knobs. Both of these approaches were a reactionary intimidation by technology, and both passed that message on to consumers. Nelson's wistful definition of the designer as the infuser of emotional content into functional objects was not much in evidence.

This design failure was certainly not unnoticed by designers themselves. At the 1989 ICSID Nagoya Congress, Ezio Manzini eloquently exhorted designers to escape from the tyranny of the size and form of the black box, and to seize opportunities offered by advances in miniaturization and integration of technologies. This message, focusing on the urgency of making products user-friendly, became a theme for design conference agendas throughout the early 1990s. Designers listened.

Now, just a few years later, there is strong evidence that Nelson's standard is becoming a reality. That evidence is, essentially, the theme for this book. New and Notable products come from designers who have recognized the importance of making the user a top priority in the planning and execution of product designs. Of the more than two thousand entries submitted for this book, approximately seventy five per cent of the product designers stated that user-friendliness was the top criterion for their design solution. Frequent references were made to ergonomic studies, user-interface design, and the importance of ease of use to design objectives. It is clear that these design objectives are understood to be the assumed tasks for the designer.

There were also many short essays among the sub-missions for this book describing the visual language the designer attempted in order to endow particular objects with an emotional trigger for users. Some of this language makes obvious reference to familiar, benign objects. Other appealing expressions are less obvious in their references.

While the intent of the designer may not always be easily interpreted—as in art, which demands that individuals bring their own experiences to the art-work—the user confronting a product of "user-centered design" is aware that there is some ambiguous, unique quality attracting them to the object. It is this intersection between designer and user that most distinguishes the designer from the engineer, the ergonomist, or the product planner. In fact, superior ergonomics and user-interface design are becoming standard requirements. It is the "soft values" that will provide the much sought after differentiation between products.

Interestingly, according to the designers featured here, many clients request design that will give their products an edge on the competition. That in itself is business as usual; marketing strategy too often continues to define itself in terms of the corporation rather than the customer. What is encouraging is that designers are taking the leadership role on behalf of the customer. This role is one we have long declared to be the vital role of the designer. They have had the courage to interpret their clients' competitive objectives in consumer-oriented terms. The products in this book are proof that designers have triumphed in preserving user-centered design in the design-to-market process.

Designer advocacy for the user was the main criterion I used for selecting the product designs included in this book. That advocacy centers on outstanding achievement of at least one of three objectives:

EASE OF USE.
Is this product physically comfortable? Can its operation be easily understood, and is it responsive to real life situations? Does it expand the power and reach of the user by improving performance or increasing knowledge?

EMOTIONAL AND CULTURAL CONTENT.
Is the product approachable and unintimidating? Does the design recall comfortable, pleasant associations with other experiences? Does it evoke traditional, cultural memories or meanings?

ENVIRONMENTAL CONSCIOUSNESS.
Is the product environmentally benign? Can it be easily recycled? Will its use have a negligible impact on the environment?

Certainly, every selected product had to meet the ease-of-use objective. Comfort, which contributes crucially to improved performance, is seriously addressed in Bill Stumpf's and Don Chadwick's Aeron Chair. ZIBA Design's Contour Keyboard for Microsoft is the essence of ergonomic correctness; it successfully addresses problems of the keyboard's comfort level and complexity. Philips Electronics' Gyroscan emphasizes its smaller size, making it more mobile for hospital-wide use.

Dramatic attention to emotional and cultural content is apparent in Emilio Ambasz's Handkerchief TV, completely changing the form and materials associated with televisions, to create a familiar, personal object. The changing character of the work environment is examined in the Citizen Office project by designers Andrea Branzi, Michele De Lucchi, and Ettore Sottsass. In imagery that blurs home and office settings, the project shifts the whole discussion about a new worklife ambience to a more emotionally referenced level. The Alessi-Philips collection of domestic appliances abandons the cool "Euro" look in favor of culturally evocative, kitchen-comfort design expression.

Environmental concerns were pursued by Michael McCoy and Dale Fahnstrom for their client, Eaglebrook Products. Since the clients themselves are in the waste recycling business, using the com-pany's collected waste material for the production of an outdoor furniture system is an elegant closing of the loop—since the furniture can also be recycled. Fitch's electric grill for Thermos offers a solution to the environmentally polluting pastime of outdoor grilling. This smaller, cleaner grill replaces the prob-lem but not the pleasure. Dictaphone Corporation's design group paid close attention to production efficiency, component replacement for extended product life, recycling, and re-use in the design of its radiology dictation system.

This book, I believe, will prove to be an important benchmark in the history of design, because it addresses user-centered issues. Rockport Publishers is to be commended for conceiving this book, not only because anthologies such as these are always valuable for providing a coherent overview of current design activities, but because it will be a per-manent record of the evolution of design.

ELECTRONICS

1

A break with the past fascination for equipment that flaunted its high-tech prowess is nearly complete. Panels bristling with rows of buttons and knobs have all but disappeared in leading-edge design. Designers are exerting a strong influence—reducing the complexity of electronic audio and video equipment to a more elegant simplicity.

Product Handkerchief TV *portable television*
Design firm Emilio Ambasz & Associates, Inc.

The design effort to bond users and their accoutrements for living into a closer relationship is demonstrated with the Handkerchief TV. The television's familiar shape and supple leather casing fit easily into a pocket. When open, the television has four planes, each incorporating a distinct function: flat screen, antenna, battery/speaker, and external ports.

VOL - |||||||

MODE

— +

Product	Signpost 101 *videophone (concept)*
Manufacturer	A T & T Global Information Solutions
Design group	A T & T Consulting Design Group
Designers	Jack Bedhun, Donald Carr

Technology for videophones is rapidly advancing. This design concept demonstrates how a single communications appliance can offer users multiple interface options. The rich variety of design imagery on the Signpost 101 expresses both its function and its flexibility

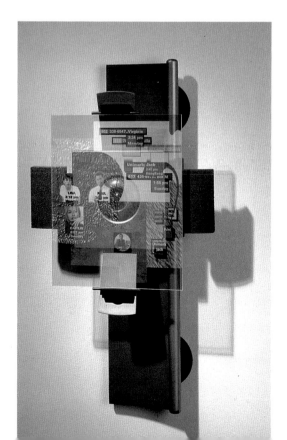

Product RL-82 Family *remote control*

Manufacturer Philips Electronics N.V.

Design firm Philips Corporate Design

Three-dimensional form gives this
simplified remote control a sleek
look and an appealing grip.

Product Sensuval *television*

Manufacturer Philips Electronics N.V.

Design firm Philips Corporate Design

A circular screen form departs from the traditional television shape, allowing the set to stand
free and occupy almost any interior space.
Sensuval's elegant, sculptural qualities
transform the television into an interior design
object to be proudly displayed.

Product **Fujitsu ICE^3** *multi-media player*

Manufacturer **Fujitsu Ltd.**

Design firm **Machineart**

Designer **Andrew Serbinski**

A compact cube design allows this unit to fit in a small space near the television. Game controllers are wireless, eliminating tangled wire chaos: storage of compact discs is incorporated into the unit's top.

Product 3-D Liquid Crystal Electronic Eyeglasses
Manufacturer Fujitsu and Imax Inc.
Design firm Kan Industrial Designers
Designer Karim Rashid

These electronic eyeglasses are synchronized
with a sensor for three-dimensional viewing.

Product IMAX® Headset *video headset*
Manufacturer IMAX
Design firm frogdesign inc.

Designed for use in an IMAX advanced technology
theater, this headset has liquid crystal lenses,
which allow the viewer to see and hear three-
dimensional movies.

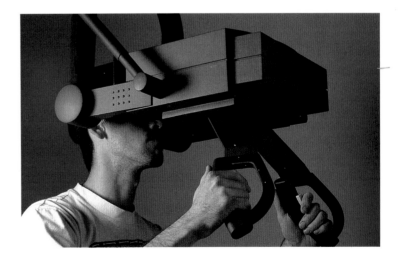

Product Virtual Combat *video game system*
Manufacturer VR-8
Design firm RKS Design, Splane Design
Designers Sean Montgomery, Bill Debley

The "virtual" interface for this game is located in the
periscope, which is meant to simulate the periscope of an
advanced combat vehicle.

Product Active Serve 73.7 cm *television monitor*
Manufacturer Sharp America
Design firm IDEO Product Development
Designer Nauto Fukasawa

This television's unusual shape is a study in contrasts: the back speaker section is hard-edged and boxy, but is punctuated with an oval front tube and soft, rounded forms for other speaker areas.

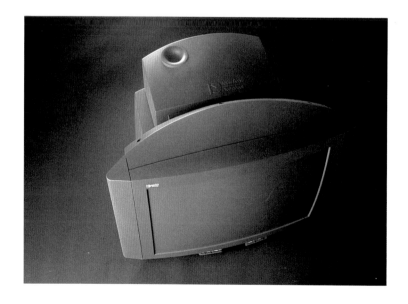

Product SEGA Compatible Video Game Controller

Manufacturer ASC II Entertainment

Design firm RKS Design, Splane Design

Designer Sean Montgomery

The ergonomic video game controller gives this product an edge in a highly competitive market. Visually, a more refined and sophisticated image appeals to today's tech-smart children and young teens.

Product Yachtboy 500, World Receiver

Manufacturer Grundig AG

Design firm Ninaber/Peters/Krowel Industrial Design

This is the newest model in a wide range of world-class receivers. The pocket size Yachtboy is the world's smallest 12-band receiver and allows listeners to tune into radio broadcasts anywhere in the world.

Product Cellular Phone
Manufacturer Mitsubishi Electric Corporation
Design firm Fitch, Inc.
Designers Deane Richardson, Keith Kreske, Mark Ciesko,
Andreas Roessner, Seiji Wada, Takanobu Fujimoto

In the contest for size reduction, this product
is among the smallest cellular phones on the
market. Its lightweight, compact design fits
easily into a pocket.

Product Virtual Reality Video Headset
Manufacturer SST
Design firm Interform
Designer Peter H. Müller

With a head-mounted display for scientific training,
and other complex uses, this video headset allows
users to experience three-dimensional interaction
in a virtual world.

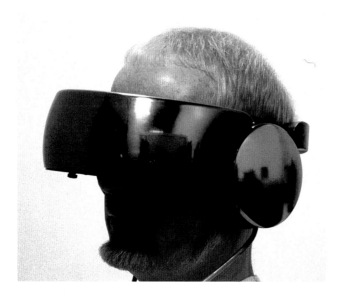

Product S3 GSM *mobile telephone*
Manufacturer Siemens AG
Design firm Siemens Design
Designers Andreas Hackbarth, Andreas Rossner

The S3 GSM is a mobile telephone
with self-explanatory interface.

Product **Home Phone** *telephone*

Manufacturer **Cicena**

Design firm **Smart Design**

Designer **Stuart Lee**

The mass-marketed Home Phone
recalls the shape of the traditional,
ubiquitous telephone, while
interpreting it in a dramatic new way.

Product **Mercury Personal Communicator**

Manufacturer **Mercury**

Design firm **IDEO**

Designers **Marc Tanner, Pete Spreenberg, Alison Black**

The size of an average human hand, this compact, easily pocketable flip phone includes a
unique button design that provides easy access
to multiple functions.

Product **Festival** *audio system*

Manufacturer Harmon/Kardon

Design firm Ashcraft Design

Designer Kurt Solland

This audio system emphasizes music enjoyment. The traditional, complex rows of buttons have been removed, and the reconfiguration and reduction of the system offers superior sound performance with simple function controls.

Product USA GOLD 777 *cellular portable telephone*

Manufacturer Omni Cellular Ltd.

Design firm Goldsmith Yamasaki Apecht Inc.

Designer Marlan H. Polhemus

A "bubble lens" and the soft contours of the enclosure are designed to make this product user-friendly.

Product Beosound Century *automatic sound system*

Manufacturer Bang & Olufsen

Designer David Lewis

Conceived as a "wall of sound," with all components (including speakers) integrated into a single, compact and uncluttered unit, the product emits beams of infrared light that sense hand movement and trigger the sliding glass doors to open. The thermoplastic cabinet is left unlacquered, so that it can be recycled.

Product · Video/Answer Image Fone 1994
videophone/answering device (concept)
Manufacturer · FUTUREWorld, Inc.
Design firm · Karim Rashid Industrial Design

The Image Fone is framed with digital imagery that is user-programmed and that displays messages.

Product   ViewCam Camcorder *video camera*

Manufacturer   Sharp Corporation

Design firm   TV & Video Systems Group. Design Center

Images recorded by ViewCam for communicating with friends or business associates can be transmitted through video modem over telephone lines. ViewCam's compact size houses a host of key new technologies.

Product Voice Communicator *(concept)*
Manufacturer EO, Inc.
Design firm IDEO
Designer Naoto Fukasawa

Capable of both voice and data transmission, the voice communicator's "tablet" and pen have a traditional design, while its handset, which nestles atop the tablet screen, is a fresh expression in handset design.

Product Personal Communicator *(concept)*
Manufacturer EO, Inc.
Design firm IDEO
Designer Naoto Fukasawa

Extending the design concepts developed for the EO Voice Communicator, a prominent fan-shaped speaker replaces this model's handset. The sleek shape and comfortable angle of the screen provide easy access for writing and speaking functions.

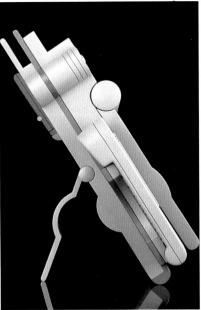

Product Phone/Fax

Manufacturer Mitsubishi Corporation

Design firm Fitch, Inc.

Designers Spencer Murrell, Gregory Breiding

This multi-featured home telecommunications product points to a design direction for future products. The number of functions (10 in all) challenged the designers to reduce the complexity for users. The solution: two "layers" that group functions according to their frequency of use.

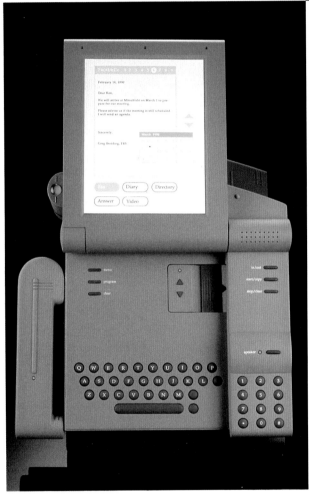

Product TP 100 Mobile Radio

Manufacturer Indelec

Design firm DOK Product Ontwerpers

Designer Gijs Ockeloen

This professional mobile radio is designed for use by police and emergency workers.

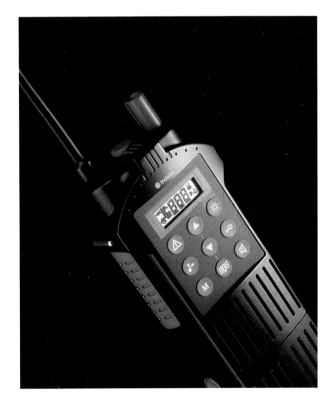

Product Home Theater Audio Show *entertainment system*
Manufacturer JBL
Design firm Fitch, Inc.
Designers Ed Lawing, Ron Vish, Tom Misage, Fitch; Sunil Mehrotra,
Herman Sperling, Alan DeVontier, JBL
Photographer Peter Rice

The quiet design aesthetic of this wireless entertainment
system makes its 16 components unobtrusive in a room.
The modular design allows portions to be stacked
vertically or horizontally.

Product Fujitsu Synapsys *multi-media player*
Manufacturer Fujitsu Ltd.
Design firm Machineart
Designers Jörg Schliefffers
Photographer Mark Jenkinson

Designed to visually express its
multiple capabilities—playing of
interactive CD ROM and video compact discs, and simple, personal
computer functions—each surface
of the machine is treated differently
for use identity. These varied visual
function triggers are integrated into
a single form.

Product HOC 8 *message machine*
Manufacturer Philips Electronics N. V.
Design group Philips Corporate Design

Philips integrates phone, fax, and answering functions
into a space-saving package for the home. The machine's
design references to stacked books and its image of the
familiar phone keep it from looking too business-like in
home interiors.

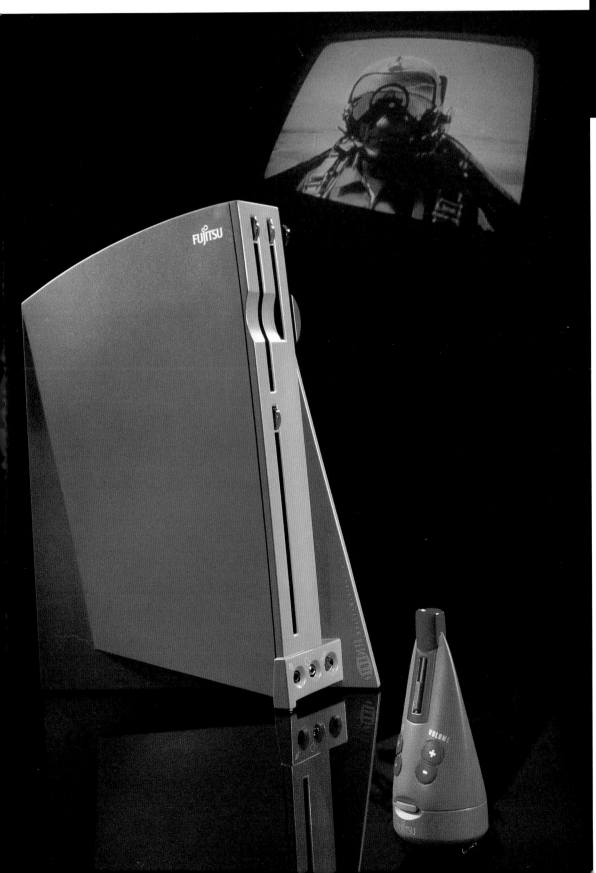

Product Second Generation *color television*
Manufacturer Samsung Electronics America
Design firm Design Continuum, Inc.
Designers John Costello, Michel Arney; Coordinator S.T. So, Samsung

This advanced design did not increase production costs, and
helped the client company re-position itself as a producer of
high-quality, high-style goods. Wide-format television technology is visually expressed in a horizontal form, while the
control panel is on top of the set, allowing for easy access
and for clutter reduction.

Product Teleconferencing Phone Module
Manufacturer Shure Brothers Inc.
Design firm Hari & Associates, Inc.
Designers Rick Mason, Victor Lazzaro

Parallel development of the phone's acoustic
chamber and its design resulted in this
triangular shape, which reduced the chamber's
size and considerably enhanced its acoustics.

Product — Auto-Telephone *car phone*
Manufacturer — Peiker Acustic
Design firm — Porsche Design GmbH
Designer — Simon Fraser

Special characteristics of this car telephone are the soft foamed-plastic grip and ear piece. The ear pad is generously proportioned to shut out external traffic noise.

Product — LCP 5000 Color LCD Projector
Manufacturer — Philips Electronics N. V.
Design firm — Philips Corporate Design

Elegance in form and significant size-reduction distinguishes this product from traditional, large, and cumbersome projectors. A new halogen system extends the life of the lamp and conserves energy.

Product   Handset for 2-Way TV
Manufacturer 2-way TV
Design firm   Hollington Associates
Designer   Peter Emrys-Roberts

Assisting subscribers of 2-way television with direct interaction with broadcast systems, this handset is used in conjunction with a graphical interface superimposed on the broadcast image. A new typology avoids the usual high-tech imagery, adopting a softer, more friendly character. The cursor control is a patented innovation.

Product   Beovision Avant *video system*
Manufacturer Bang & Olufsen A/S
Designer   David Lewis

The manufacturer, long respected for design classicism in audio and video products, maintains a consistent signature of sophisticated elegance in adapting wide-screen technology to its new video system.

Product	Calida TV set
Manufacturer	Loewe
Design firm	Phoenix Product Design

The sculptural quality of the Calida television turns away from the technical language of traditional television design.

Product Taihan DCP Telephone

Manufacturer Taihan Electric Wire Co.

Design firm Lunar Design

Designers Jeff Smith, Yves Behar, Brett Lovelady, Andrew Zee, Gerard Furbershaw

The design language of this product, with its asymmetrical and flattened shape, departs from the popular, generic forms for wireless telephones.

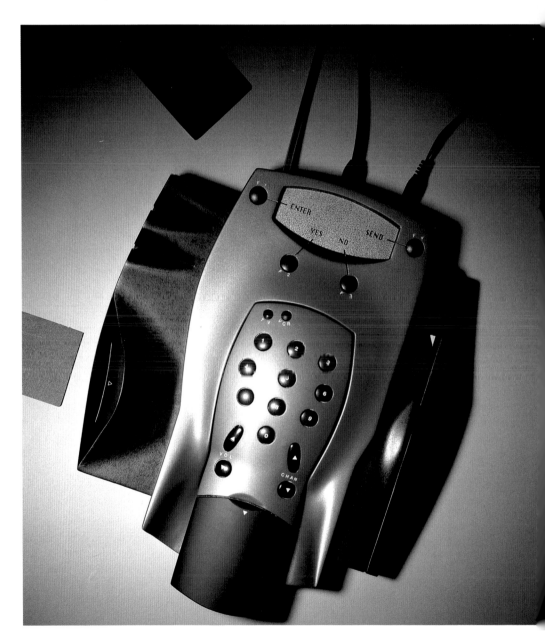

Product Focus *home shopping assistant*

Manufacturer Tandem Computers

Design firm Tandem Industrial Design Group

Designer Trung Phung

The product assists home shoppers ordering merchandise through television.

Product **CDF-100 Portable Photo Compact Disc Player**

Manufacturer **Philips Electronics N.V.**

Design firm **Philips Corporate Design**

This easy-to-operate equipment allows photographs stored on photo compact discs to be shown on any television screen or computer monitor. The design is based on the image of a camera.

Product **Pager Phone**

Manufacturer **Universal Cellular**

Design firm **Taylor & Chu**

Designer **Robin Chu**

The 13.7- by -6.6 cm combination phone/pager is designed with a cover case that slides and expands to the size of a standard phone.

Product **GSM Phone**

Manufacturer **Nokia Mobile Phones Ltd.**

Design firm **E & D Design**

Designers **Taponi Hyvonen, Tomek Rudkiewicz**

The size reduction of this phone does not sacrifice clarity in the layout and function of the keypad. This is an example of how design can simplify the complex technology of multi-function products.

Product Car Audio and Environment Controls

Manufacturer Mercedes Benz

Designer Bruno Zacco

The designers took a fresh approach to the rectangular slot/control panel found in most cars. The graceful double ellipses and the use of leather suggest a return to the elegant interior details of vintage auto-styling.

Product Angelo *wireless phone*

Manufacturer Genesis technologies

Design firm frogdesign inc.

This wireless phone, with its three-color design and geometric shape, sits as a piece of art on any home or office surface.

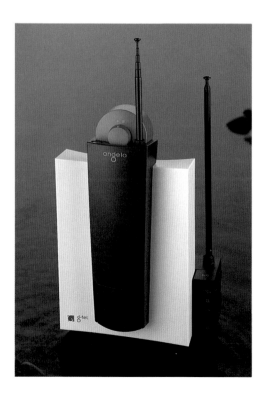

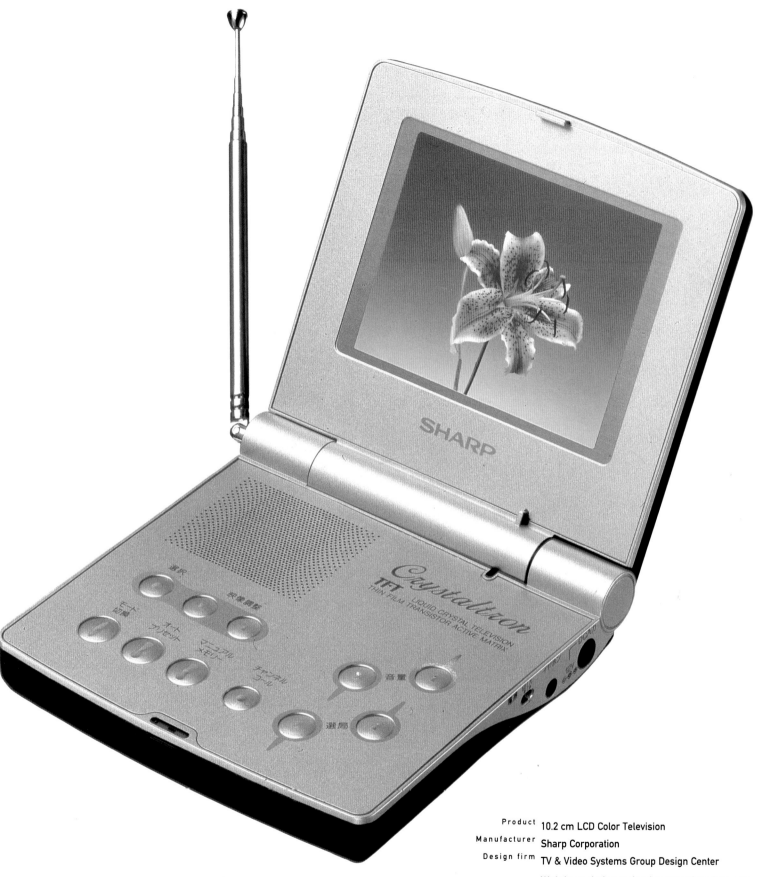

Product 10.2 cm LCD Color Television

Manufacturer Sharp Corporation

Design firm TV & Video Systems Group Design Center

Weight and size reduction translate into one of the slimmest-profile portable televisions available. The compact and lightweight LCD fits easily into small spaces such as pockets.

Product Voiceman *karaoke system*

Manufacturer Pioneer Corporation

Design firm ZIBA Design, Inc.

Designers Jan Hippen, Henry Chin

This streamlined Karaoke laser disc system's
two components are some of the smallest
on the market and can store easily in most
living rooms.

Product Aplicom DT 3000 Mobile Terminal *automotive
communications system*

Manufacturer Computec OY

Design firm E & D Design

Designers Heikki Salo, Robert Hellier, Matti Koivisto

The mobile terminal is a wireless communications and data transmission
system for numerous kinds of service operations. It has been designed for
use in demanding situations for simplicity and reliable performance.

Product Automotive Radar Detector

Manufacturer Valentine Research

Design firm Design Central

Designers Joe Juratovac, Dave Roche

The unit sends signals multidirectionally and incorporates an innovative angle-adjustment system that provides accurate radar detection.

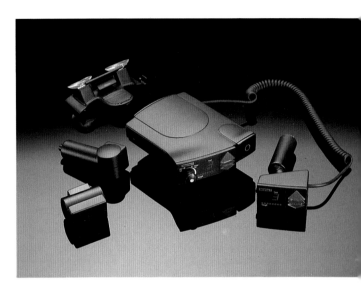

Product Beosystem AV 9000 *television*

Manufacturer Bang & Olufsen A/S

Designer David Lewis

Two features, one aesthetic and the other functional, give this product distinction. The black polycarbonate foil cover slides away from the television screen when the set is turned on, a metaphor for the parting of a cinema curtain. The functional design of the system's automatic set-up and calibration eliminates hours of tedious labor.

LIGHTING

2

Product Lampadina *floor lamp*
Manufacturer Yamada Shomei Lighting Co., Ltd.
Design firm Igarashi Studio
Designer Takenobu Igarashi

Delicate translucent shades of bone china create quarter,
half, and full "moons" that can be adjusted as desired to
direct pools of light.

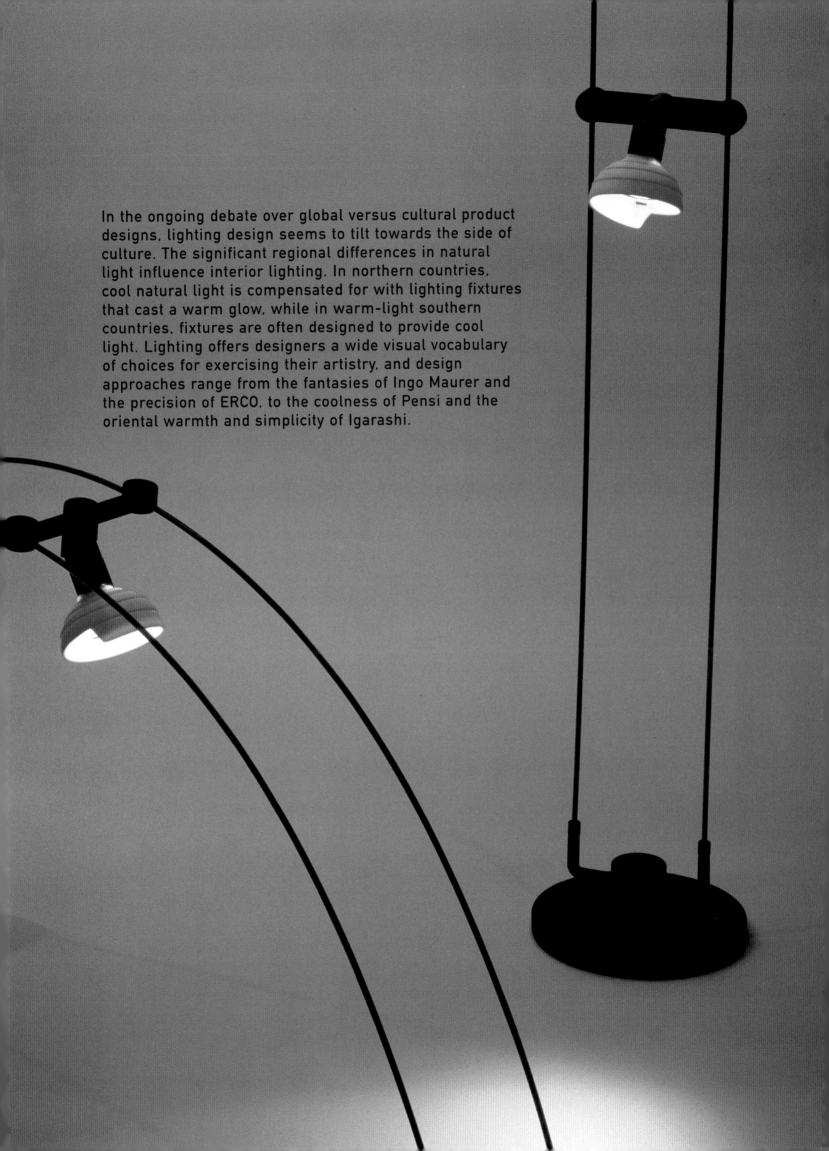

In the ongoing debate over global versus cultural product designs, lighting design seems to tilt towards the side of culture. The significant regional differences in natural light influence interior lighting. In northern countries, cool natural light is compensated for with lighting fixtures that cast a warm glow, while in warm-light southern countries, fixtures are often designed to provide cool light. Lighting offers designers a wide visual vocabulary of choices for exercising their artistry, and design approaches range from the fantasies of Ingo Maurer and the precision of ERCO, to the coolness of Pensi and the oriental warmth and simplicity of Igarashi.

Product   Pollux *low-voltage spotlight*
Manufacturer   ERCO Leuchten GmbH
Design group   ERCO Design

This modular lamp concept includes accessories to produce a variety of different lighting effects: from sharp-edged beams to gobo projections and moire patterns.

Product   Hot Achille *ceiling lamp*
Manufacturer   Ingo Maurer GmbH
Design firm   Ingo Maurer GmbH
Designers   Ingo Maurer and team

This lamp is suitable for ceiling heights of up to three meters. An adjustable weight ensures that the coaxial cable remains taut, while the stainless steel luminary elements float elegantly in space.

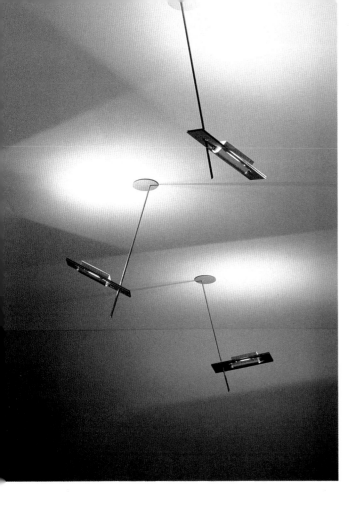

Product **Wandering Finger** *ceiling lamp*

Manufacturer **Ingo Maurer GmbH**

Design firm **Ingo Maurer GmbH**

Designer **Ingo Maurer**

This stainless steel "finger" lamp is designed to provide indirect light. The reflector is fitted with a ball-and-socket joint, making it freely adjustable.

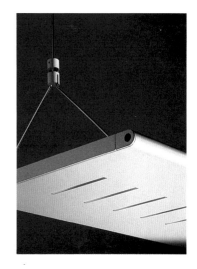

Product **Skylight** *suspended light fixture*

Manufacturer **Luxo Italiana S.p.A.**

Design firm **Neostudio Di R. Lanciani & W. Posern**

A system of suspended luminaries provides uplighting, downlighting, and ambient light effects.

Product **Stella** *compact projector*

Manufacturer **ERCO Leuchten GmbH**

Designer **Franco Clivio**

Borrowing a technique that has long been used in stage lighting, this projector lamp uses the combined effects of light and materials to project concise images. Stella compact projectors are designed for everyday use and will fit in most rooms of normal dimensions.

Product Fenix *halogen lamp*
Manufacturer Garciá Garay SL
Design firm Garciá Garay SL
Designer J. Garciá Garay

This halogen fixture reflects light from the painted metal canopies located above the bulb.

Product Sinova *floor lamp*
Manufacturer Siemens AG
Design Group Siemens Design

The graceful column, with its step-molded vertical markings, recalls Classical Greek architecture. The flattened elliptical shape, however, is an unexpected form that gives the lamp a contemporary character.

Product Enterprise *halogen lamp*
Manufacturer Garciá Garay SL
Design firm Garciá Garay SL
Designer J. Garciá Garay

Variable effects are created with this halogen fixture, which reflects light from its moveable wings.

Product **Belys** *lighting system*

Manufacturer Vanlux, S.A.

Designer Jorge Pensi

This system incorporates table, floor, and hanging fixtures with white polycarbonate diffusers, as well as multi-colored accent rims.

Product Lobby adjustable lamp

Manufacturer Vanlux S.A.

Designer Jorge Pensi

This system of white-sanded polycarbonate light diffusers is designed to create different lighting effects for wall- or rail-mounted lights, and for continuous linear hanging lamps.

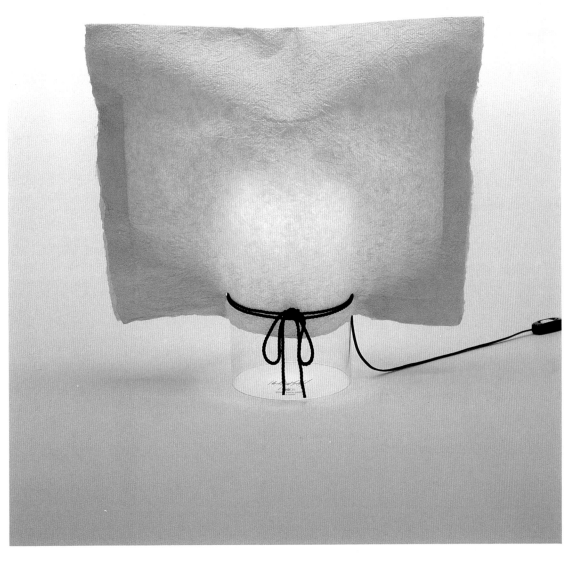

Product Zukin *table lamp*

Manufacturer Yamada Shomei Lighting Co., Ltd.

Design firm Igarishi Studio

Designer Takenobu Igarashi

A contemporary version of sixteenth century bamboo and paper lamp designs, this lamp's handmade paper shade fits over a glass tube and is tied in place.

Product Regina *adjustable lamp*

Manufacturer B.Lux S.A.

Designer Jorge Pensi

This lamp's carbonate shade in blue, pale green, and lilac is mounted on dual stems for adjustability.

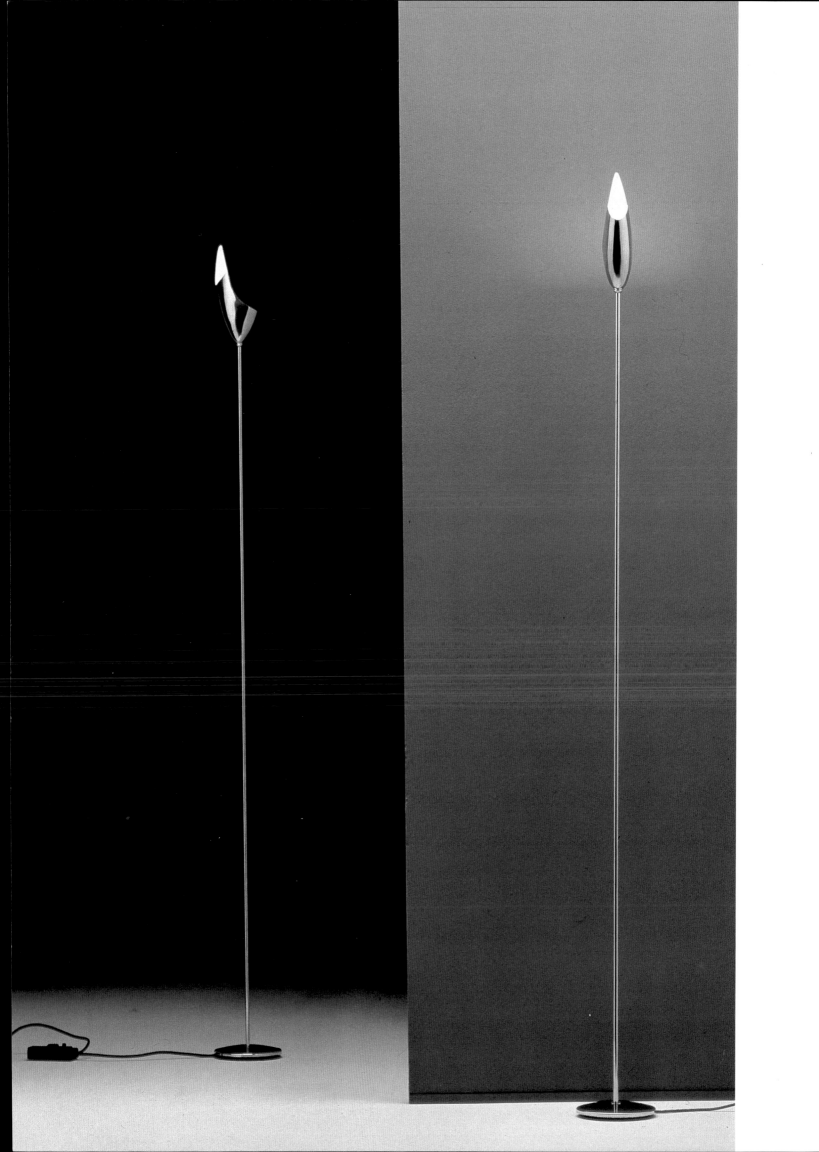

Product Dulcinea *table lamp*
Manufacturer GFA Los Angeles
Design firm Karim Rashid Industrial Design
Designer Karim Rashid

The tulip-shaped design of this table lamp in yellow glass and brass appears to float in a dark room.

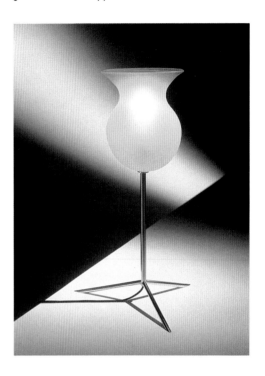

Product Alys *floor lamp*
Manufacturer Vanlux S.A.
Designer Jorge Pensi

The white-sanded, carbonate light diffuser has petals of the same materials colored white, pale green, and lilac, and mounted on a thin chrome shaft like a budding flower.

Product Delft *wall lamp*
Manufacturer Ryan & Associates
Design firm Ryan & Associates
Designer David Ryan

Energy efficient through the use of fluorescent bulbs, Delft wall lamps capture and frame light like the archetypal giver of light, the window. This fixture can be hung like a picture or plugged into a socket.

Product Servul *floor lamp*

Manufacturer Flos S.P.A.

Design firm Josep Lluscà Disseny Industrial SL

Designer Josep Lluscà

The lamp can be wall-mounted or used as a torchier: its painted metal base has a bright red accent, visually anchoring the piece.

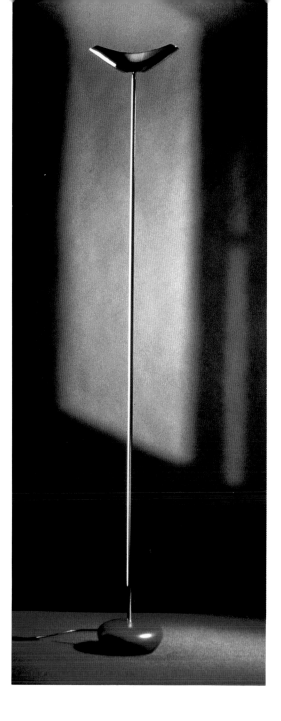

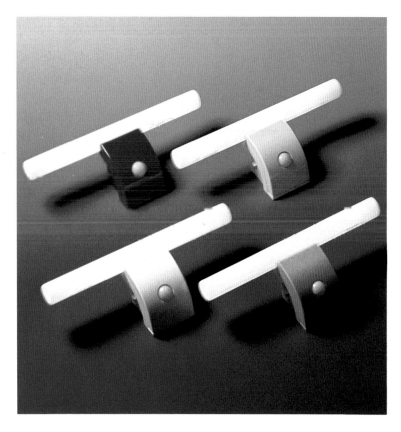

Product Innen *sensor lamp*

Manufacturer Steinel GmbH

Design firm Lou Beeren Industrial Design

This interior lamp is fitted with an infrared sensor that measures heat and then responds by turning on the light. The sensor lamp design also includes an automatic on-off control.

Product **Porca Miseria** *chandelier*
Manufacturer **Ingo Maurer GmbH**
Design firm **Ingo Maurer GmbH**
Designer **Ingo Maurer**

Challenging today's conservative chandelier trends, designer
Ingo Maurer incorporated the image of a slow-motion explo-
sion in the design of this porcelain fixture.

Product Sunset *outdoor lighting*

Manufacturer Lampas

Designer Peter Pysted

This is a sophisticated yet rugged bollard light that provides directed light to outdoor spaces.

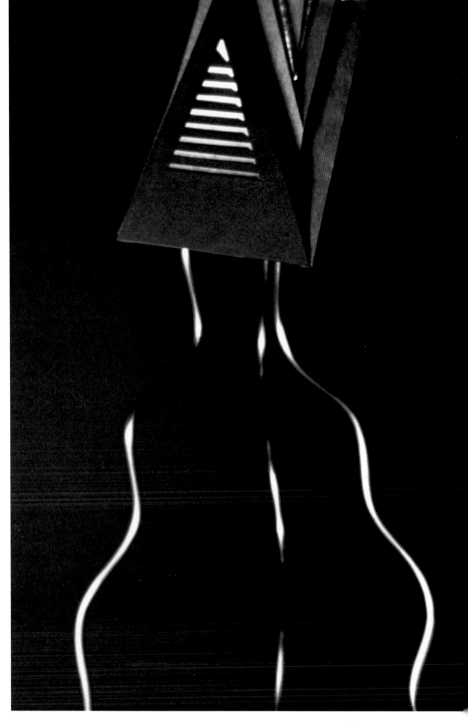

Product Nocturne *floor lamp (concept)*

Designer Linda A. Kuo

This 16.5 dm floor lamp seems to have its own spirit; in dim lighting, the lamp casts a warm glow and appears to dance on the floor.

Product Beacon Vilanova *street light*

Manufacturer Diseño Ahorro Energético SA (DAE)

Designer Leopoldo Milà

This street light is cast in aluminum with circular frames that divide and disperse the light.

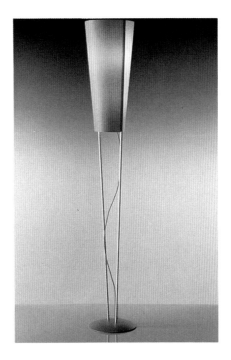

Product — Hermes *table lamp*
Manufacturer — Luxo Italiano S.p.A.
Designer — Architect Francesco Lucchese

This piece casts a soft pastel light and stands as a sculpture, with its multicolored shade suspended between two thin columns.

Product — Heron *table lamp*
Manufacturer — Luxo Italiana S.p.A
Design — Architect Isao Hosoe

Designed in six strong colors, these flexible yet sturdy lamps add both a splash of color and directed light to any room.

Product **Beacon Augusta** *outdoor wall light*
Manufacturer **Diseño Ahorro Energético SA (DAE)**
Designers **A. Ferrer, J. Auge, A. Viscasillas**

Cast-aluminum wall lighting adds durability to a new concept in illumination, based on the task of visually improving design for urban environments.

Product **Andrea** *street light*
Manufacturer **Diseno Ahorro Energetico SA (DAE)**
Designers **Martorell, Bohigas, MacKay**

These street lights, designed for the Barcelona Olympic site, are monumental in their columnar and detailed design.

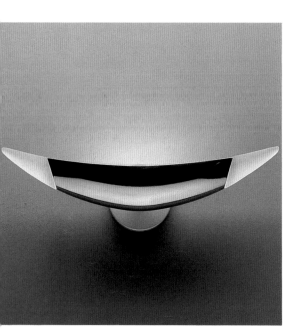

Product **Horus** *halogen wall fixture*
Manufacturer **B.Lux S.A.**
Designer **Jorge Pensi**

The wall-mounted halogen fixture with its polished metal has carbonate shades in variable cool colors.

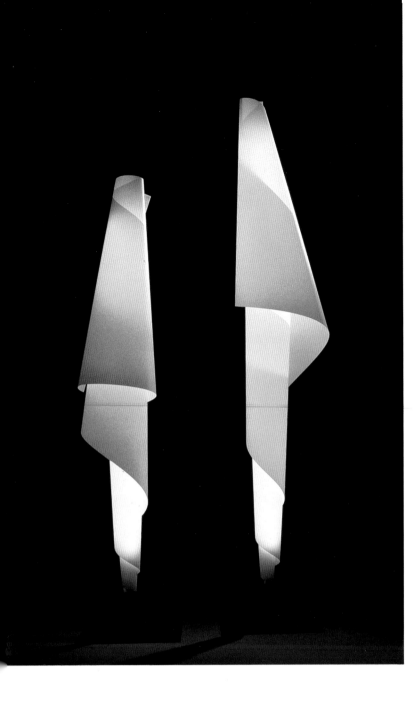

Product   Costura *floor lamp*
Manufacturer   Metalarte, S.A.
Designer   Josep Aregall

This floor lamp has a black lacquered metal column with a white opalescent diffuser. The on/off switch is located on the cord, to avoid interrupting the upward movement of the design.

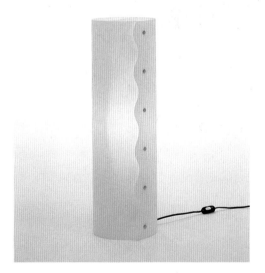

Product   Nami *table lamp*
Manufacturer   Yamada Shomei Lighting Co., Ltd.
Design firm   Igarashi Studio
Designer   Takenobu Igarashi

The Nami waron plate is rolled to form an s-shaped cylinder, which is held in position with snaps, created with minimal materials, light in weight, and requires no tools for assembly. This lamp is both environment- and user-friendly.

TOOLS FOR
LIVING

3

Exciting new designs for household products represent
a break with the crisp, precision-edged vocabulary of
Eurodesign. The New Tools concept and the Philips-Alessi
Line are examples of a bold, new exploration into the
emotional content of design. These designs bring a human
dimension to form and function by endowing products with
a personality that encourages user involvement. The
evidence of this more human-directed dialogue is also
apparent in new designs for personal care and home care.

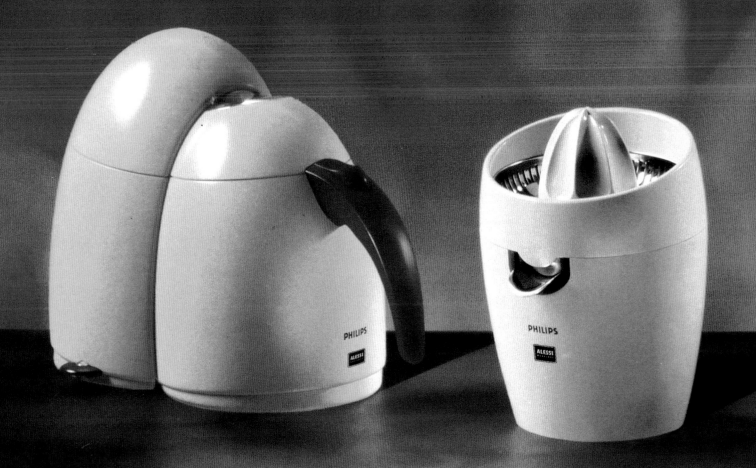

Product	Philips-Alessi Line *cooking appliances*
Manufacturer	Philips Electronics N.V.
Design groups	Philips Corporate Design, Alessi Design
Project Consultant	Alessandro Mendini

This collaborative design effort sought to restore balance between human warmth and high tech convenience in kitchen appliances. Non-intrusive pastel colors, high quality materials, and advanced technology make these products a reliable addition to the kitchen.

(Photo-left to right) Twin-dome coffeemaker; Citrus Press; Toaster; and Hot Water Kettle.

PHILIPS

Product   Soft-Side Coolers
Manufacturer Thermos Company
Design firm   Fitch Inc.
Designers   Keith Kreske, Gregory Breiding

Extensive market research
revealed a demand for cool and
dry storage combined in a single bag. A rugged, soft-molded
bottom for beverages, and a
soft, insulated top are supple-
mented with a variety of outside
pockets for stowing beach or
sport clothing. The coolers are
lightweight and compress
easily for storage.

Product   Plastic Film Dispenser
Manufacturer W. Ralston (Canada) Inc.
Design firm   The Axis Group Inc.
Designers   Alexander Manu, Harry Mahler

This plastic film dispenser uses a studded rubber base and a sharp
cutting edge to solve the problem of stuck-together film.

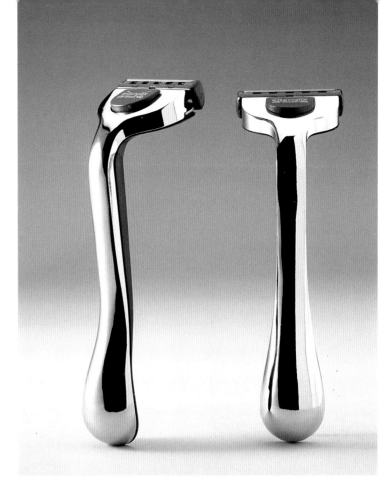

Product Philishave HS 190 *battery shaver*

Manufacturer Philips Electronics N.V.

Design firm Philips Corporate Design

The beautifully contoured shape of this compact shaver fits the hand, while the soft, highly tactile plastic case feels pleasantly like a second skin. The shaver's simple, seductive form belies the complex mechanism within. With three weeks of cordless power supply residing in its two batteries and a reengineered transmission, this is truly a high-performance portable shaver.

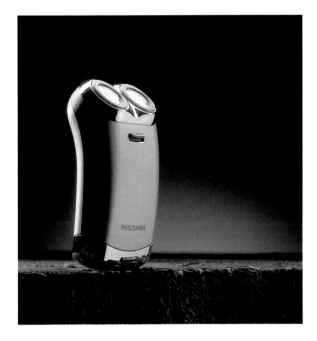

Product Protector *razor*

Manufacturer Wilkinson Sword

Design firm Pentagram Design Ltd.

Designers Kenneth Grange, Gavin Thomson

Sleek in its chromed metal cloak, this shaver presents a leap forward in user benefits. A network of fine wires wound across the cutting edge of the blade offers protection from nicks and cuts. Soft, circular pads on the weighted handle add to the sense of security.

Product Philishave Rota 93 *battery shaver*

Manufacturer Philips Electronics N.V.

Design firm Philips Corporate Design

Friendly interaction with the user is characterized by the Philishave Rota's indicator feature, which reports the amount of shaving time left on the battery and when it's time for a cleaning. Soft side panels and soft-touch lacquer endow the hand-contoured form with a very pleasing "feel". Both the Philishave and its packaging meet the manufacturer's environmental "three R's" policy: Reduce, Re-use, and Recycle.

Product Electric Water Kettle 0.81

Manufacturer BODUM AG

Design firm PI-DESIGN AG

Designer Charlotte Warming

Fresh and clean-lined, the cheerful red color of this kettle signals the purpose of the appliance, while the bright green switch can be quickly identified.

Product New Tools *cooking appliances (concept)*

Commissioner Philips Electronics N.V.

Designers Marco Susani, Mario Trimarchi

Commissioned as a project to explore new concepts for kitchen tools, these appliances reflect widespread interest in traditional "cultural" food preparation. Thus, while New Tools are simple both in their form and function, the evocative use of traditional materials and forms presents a refreshing new approach to cooking appliances.

Product FlashBake Oven

Manufacturer Quadlux, Inc.

Design firm Lunar Design

Designers David Laituri, Max Yoshimoto, Gerard Furbershaw

Introduction of a new cooking technology called for a design that would attract attention to the oven's leading edge, patented process. The undulating shape in a bright, stainless steel exterior sitting atop four, round sturdy legs is a new visual presentation for countertop ovens.

Product **1200 Series Carafe** *thermos*

Manufacturer **Thermos Company**

Design firm **Fitch Inc.**

Designers **Bob Mervar, Gregory Breiding, Mark Ciesco**

The 1200 Series Carafe offers a low-cost contemporary design. The carafe, available in a six- and eight-cup size, features a break-proof, vacuum-insulated, stainless steel liner.

Product   Prima *electric coffeemaker*
Manufacturer   F et B Research
Design firm   Frechin et Bureaux

Taking a minimalist approach to coffeemaker design, the Prima is an elegant object whose function is speculative when the unit is closed. The color is a new and unusual application to kitchen appliances.

Product   Electric Grill
Manufacturer   Thermos Company
Design firm   Fitch Inc.
Designers   Andreas Roessner, Dale Benedict, Susan Haller, Gregory Breiding, Mark Ciesco

Designed for use in limited space, this elliptical grill not only has a reduced footprint, its insulated dome and high-performance cooking surface make it environmentally superior to conventional grills. A number of design features also make the grill suitable for tableside use.

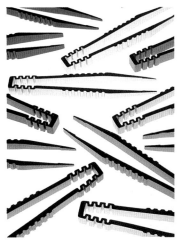

Product Bissell Plus *upright vacuum system*

Manufacturer Bissell Inc.

Design firm Bissell Industrial Design Group

Designers Steven Umbach, James Weaver, Giovanni Pino
Mark Zuiderveen

This product represents an innovative leap by combining the functions of uprights with on-board accessory tools, cannisters, and small clean-up portables. By simply releasing a latch, the light weight cannister lifts off as a portable cleaner for small jobs.

Product Tweezers

Manufacturer Pressweld (UK) Ltd.

Design firm Ryan & Associates

Designer David Ryan

The range of colors in a usually utilitarian-looking object, along with a ridged grip, transforms these tweezers from the ordinary into something new and refreshing.

Product Wave *bathroom scale*
Manufacturer Polder
Design firm Smart Design, Inc.
Designer Stuart Harey Lee

The design of this scale employs the fluid image of liquid with a waved surface, coinciding with the bathing theme. A red dial makes weight measurements easy to read.

Product Aero *hair dryer*
Manufacturer Remmington
Design firm Smart Design
Designer David Peschel
Photographer George Larkins

A physiognomic handle and aerodynamic form combine to give this hair dryer power and practical storage ability.

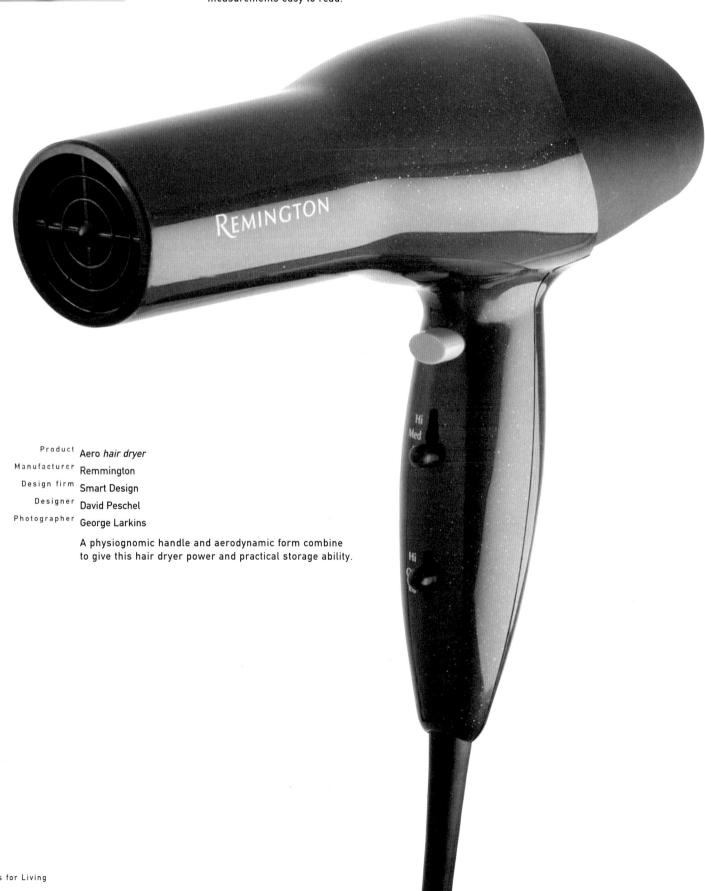

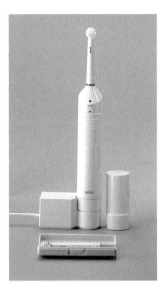

Product   Plak Control Travel *electric toothbrush*
Manufacturer   Braun AG
Design group   Braun Design Department
Designer   Peter Hartwein

Keeping this unit protected, yet portable enough
for travel, was a design priority. The lightweight
plastic housing is safely watertight, and a protective cap prevents damage. The unit fits neatly
inside its case, which has perforations for air
circulation.

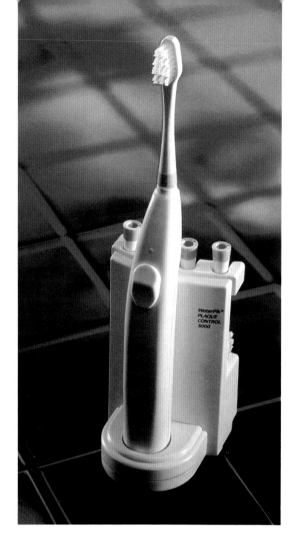

Product   Teledyne Water Pik PC3000 *plaque control instrument*
Manufacturer   Teledyne Water Pik
Design firm   Machineart
Designers   Andrew Serbinski, S. Bellofatto, M. Turchi

Designed for an international market, the Waterpik's
design focuses on achieving an "expression of performance that is inviting to experience." The handle
has a flat back surface to prevent rolling when placed
on a counter. Minimizing the shelf space needed for
storage was also an important design consideration.

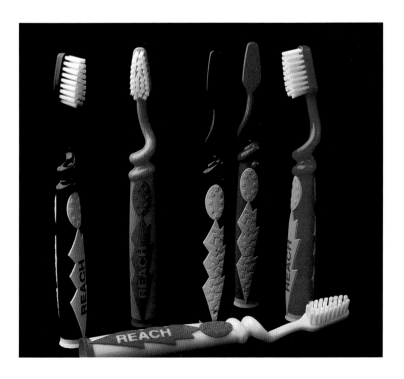

Product   Wonder Grip *children's toothbrush*
Manufacturer   Johnson and Johnson
Design firm   Smart Design
Designers   Dan Formosa (ergonomics), Ric Norregaard

Is it possible to make brushing teeth fun for kids? Wonder
Grip's bright handle is sized to fit small hands and is designed
to make it "cool" for kids to brush their teeth.

Product Vacuum Cleaner

Manufacturer Moulinex

Design firm Lou Beeren Industrial Design

The compact design of this vacuum cleaner
makes it easy to store, as well as giving it
efficient power for high utility.

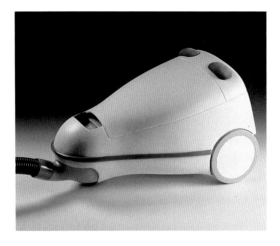

Product Feddy Mops

Manufacturer Duskin

Design firm Fitch Inc.

Designers Deane Richardson, Frank Wilgus, David Laiture

These well-designed mops bring a sophisticated
appearance, new materials, and user-friendly
design to a standard household cleaning product.

Product Triathlon *floor cleaner*

Manufacturer Philips Electronics N.V.

Design group Philips Corporate Design

Total floor cleaning for a variety of surfaces and materials,
including the integration of vacuum cleaner and shampoo
functions, make this an efficient machine. Attention is paid to
both ergonomic and ecologic features. Nearly all components
are recyclable, as is the packaging. The pear shape of
Triathlon contributes to easier maneuverability.

Product   O'Cedar 2000 Line *cleaning tools*

Manufacturer   O'Cedar/Vining Company

Design firm   Design Central

Designers   Diana Woehnl Juratovac, Rainer Teufel, Tim Friar, John Koenig, Peter Koloski

Each product in this line has a large diameter and a heavy-duty metal handle with a ribbed plastic coating for an improved grip. The sponge mop is injection-molded, rust-free, and has no sharp edges. The dust mop is dual-sided and includes an angle-flex head. The broom has dual and heavy bristles for various sweeping jobs.

Product **Revere Excel** *cookware*

Manufacturer **Corning**

Design firm **Ecco Design, Inc.**

Designers **Eric Chan, Jeff Miller, Fede Carandini**

These premium products incorporate new features while preserving the established Revere look. Knobs and handles have large surfaces and a recessed dot pattern to provide a better grip.

Product **ToastMan** *toaster*

Manufacturer **Design Edge**

Design firm **Design Edge**

The palm-sized toaster is a space and time-saver. Its thermo-electric heating element toasts a slice of bread in just 45 seconds.

Product **Espresso Machine**
Manufacturer **Philips Electronics N.V.**
Designers **Philips Corporate Design and**
Lou Beeren Industrial Design

The espresso ritual in Italy is like the opera: dramatic, a big populist event. This machine is a stage set for making espresso, presenting the coffee in a dramatic way, with an appliance at a reasonable cost.

Product **Electric Coffeemaker**
Manufacturer **Philips Electronics N.V.**
Designers **Philips Corporate Design and**
Lou Beeren Industrial Design

In this design, the typical European cylindrical container shape is discarded for an hourglass form. The coffeemaking process is still evident, but the softer shape is warm and inviting.

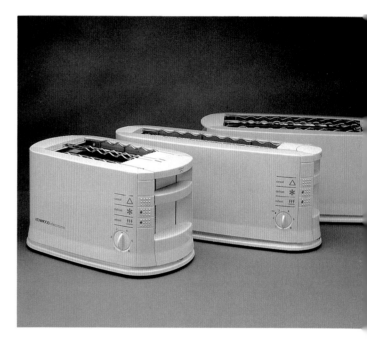

Product **Toaster**
Manufacturer **Kenwood Ltd.**
Design firm **Pentagram Design Ltd.**
Designers **Kenneth Grange, Peter Foskett**

A swing-up rack for warming buns and bread, and a liftable bread carriage for smaller items are features of this sleek, curved toaster.

Product Aliseu *ceiling fan*

Manufacturer Singer do Brazil

Design firm Neumeister Design and NCS Design Rio

Designers Alexander Neumeister, Celso Santos, Angela Carvalho

This product is a refreshing change from traditional ceiling fans. Injection molding considerably reduces the weight of the roof ventilator, while easy-to-install blades click into place and require no further adjustment.

Product Bathroom Range

Manufacturer Duravit AG

Design firm Phiippe Starck, Paris

Back-to-basics is expressed in this range through the metaphor of the shallow bowl—reminiscent of the water bucket first used in personal hygiene functions. A wooden base adds a warm tone to the bath, while the slim, tall faucet fixture draws the eye upward.

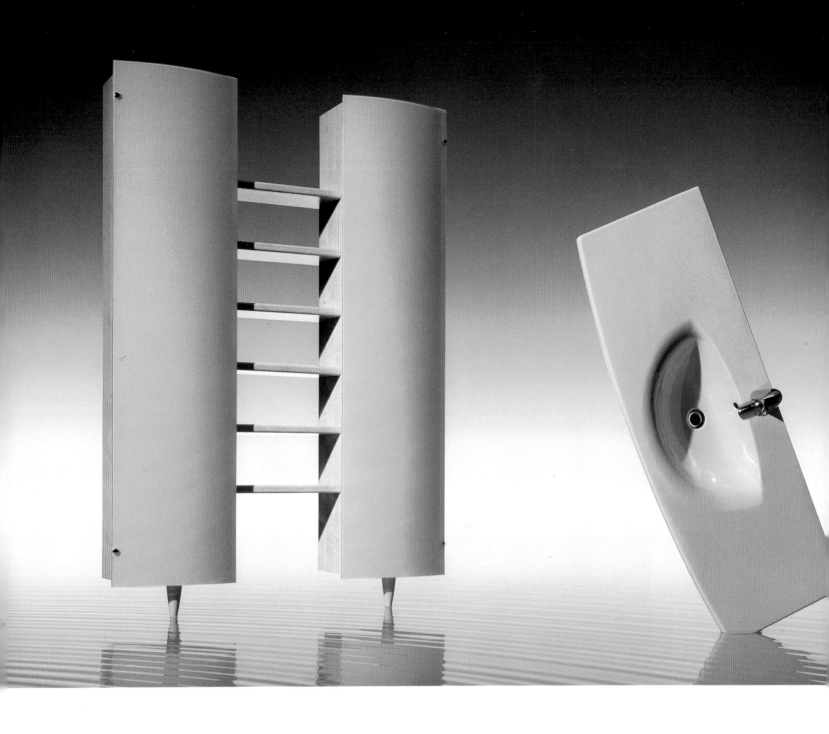

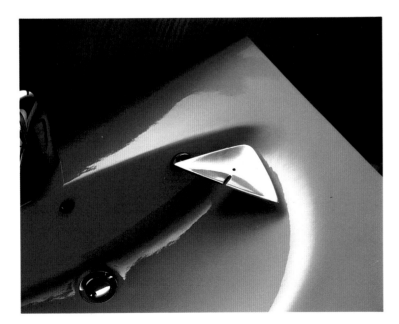

Product **Caro *bathroom range***

Manufacturer Duravit

Design firm Phoenix Product Design

Reductive design gives this range a simplicity that expresses near-asceticism. Even the cabinet handles are eliminated, replaced with a matte, sandblasted glass material that also hides fingerprints.

Product Plastic Bowls

Manufacturer Rosti Housewares

Designer Ole Palsby

Textured plastic and vibrant colors give a jewel-like translucence to these elegant bowls. Built-in handles make these products easy to pick up and carry.

Product Primo *orange juice maker*

Manufacturer F et B Research

Design firm Frechin et Bureaux

An interesting combination of metal and plastic, the Primo handheld juicer offers ease-of-use and attractive design in a non-traditional color.

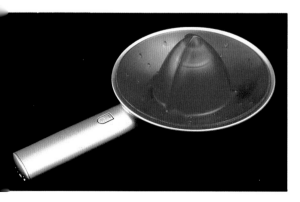

Product Bathroom Faucet

Design firm Priority Designs

Designer Paul Kolada

A postmodern image for a practical product, this black faucet set adds a dramatic twist to the bathroom sink. Simple, primary red and blue color splashes indicate handles for hot and cold water.

Product Oras Vienda Water Mixers

Manufacturer Oras OY

Design firm E & D Design OY

Designer Jorma Vennola

This range of bathroom and kitchen faucets combines beauty with function. The hollow ring handle provides easy temperature and pressure control.

HEALTHCARE

4

Product Integrated Brachy Unit *X-ray system*
Manufacturer Nucletron Research BV
Design firm dok Produktontwerpers
Designers Gijs Ockeloen, Mauritz De Koning

The design of this X-ray therapy system and cantilevered patient lorry integrates technical and human factors in its construction.

The design of medical and laboratory equipment is concerned, at the minimum, with life and death situations and, at the maximum, with patient comfort and psychological well-being. In addition, there is the challenge to help the patient feel more comfortable during the process of diagnostics, surgery, and aftercare. In the past, appearance has very often been ignored in favor of technical function.

A new focus on design has begun to improve medical and laboratory equipment. Stringent ergonomic and user-interface design standards are also fostering change, causing the designers to seriously address the efficiency and potential for errors in the interface between the equipment and medical personnel.

Without losing sight of the serious nature of this equipment, the designer still has an opportunity to endow it with elegance of form, adding legitimate, visual nobility to the function of the equipment.

Product   Gyroscan NT System *magnetic resonance system*
Manufacturer   Philips Electronics N. V.
Design firm   Philips Corporate Design

This scanner is among the smallest and lightest in its class. The form language of waves gives the illusion of a slimmer profile and also creates the comforting image of two cradling hands. The newly-integrated liquid crystal display (LCD) allows a closer relationship between technician and patient. The design includes all elements in the scanner environment, including work stations, cabinets, and other necessary mouse-driven controls and equipment.

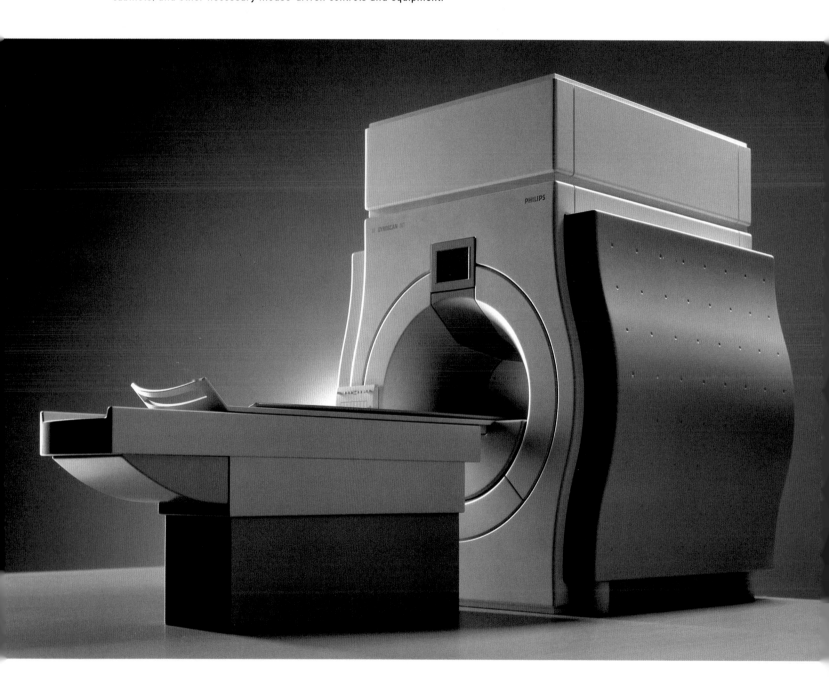

Product **Home Pill Dispenser**
Manufacturer **Alnamar Inc.**
Design firm **ZIBA Design Inc.**
Designer **Mark Stella**

At the push of the button this dispenser releases a pre-measured dosage of pills into a removable cup. The dispenser opens like a book for easy refilling.

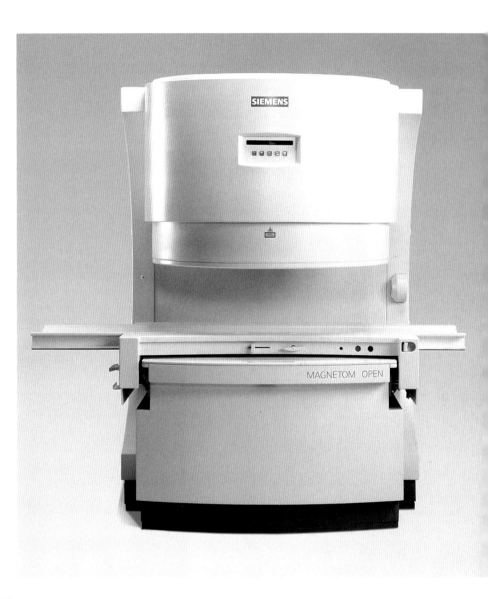

Product **Magnetom Open** *magnetic resonance diagnostic equipment*
Manufacturer **Siemens AG**
Design group **Siemens Design**
Designer **Hatto Grosse**

Patient anxiety and comfort are addressed in the design of this unit by abandoning the traditional tunnel format, allowing patients to lie in an open space, where they have contact with medical personnel and escape the trapped feeling of lying in an enclosed tunnel. Constructed by placing two magnets above one another, with an open space between in which the patient lies, the design employs wood, rather than plastic, housing the magnets, to further reduce the intimidating look of this equipment.

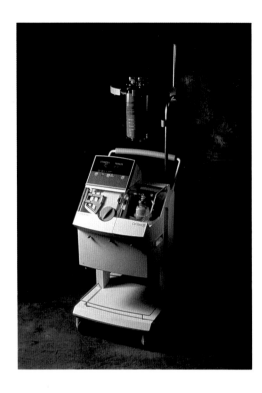

Product   Cellsaver 5 *blood collection system*

Manufacturer Haemonetics Corporation

Design firm   Design Continuum Inc.

Designers   Stephen Guerrera, Betsy Goodrich, Richard Miller, Tim Dearborn, Jack Grundlach, Joe Geringer (Design Continuum Inc.), Gary Stacey, Russ Herrig (Haemonetics Corporation)

This system collects a patient's blood during surgery and cleans and packs it for reinfusion to the patient. The new design improves the system's ergonomics for both standing and seated operators. The tubing layout is redesigned to fall naturally into place, while tubing and bags are color-coded for easy grouping. Other design improvements include a simplified key pad, easy-to-clean parts, and a time-saving setup.

Product   Versapulse Select *surgical laser*

Manufacturer Coherent, Inc.

Design firm   Lunar Design

Designers   Max Yoshimoto, Gil Wong, Bjarki Hallgrimmson, Gerard Furbershaw, Marieke Van Wijnen

This surgical laser device is designed to reduce invasive operating procedures, communicate value, quality, and long product life, and meet user-interface demands. The equipment rolls easily from one surgical suite to another, and the sterile, handheld laser attachment can be changed for individual procedures.

Product Sirona C1 *dental treatment station*
Manufacturer Siemens AG
Design firm Siemens Design
Designers Tilman Phelps, Klaus Stockl

All functions incorporated in this unit can be controlled either by hand using the display or with a foot-operated mouse, leaving the dentist two free hands. The smooth generously dimensioned surfaces express clarity of control.

Product Disposable Surgeon's Thimble
Manufacturer Bissell Medical Products Inc.
Design firm Montgomery Design International
Designers Jim Voorheis, Douglas Montgomery, Robert Rajsky

The increasing problem of transmission of disease to medical personnel through inadvertent needle pricks gave impetus to the design of this product. The thimble is sculpted in an inverted cone at its end, which leads the needle to a wedge trap at the bottom of the cone. A flexible silicone joint between the thimble and its gripping handle allows easier manipulation of the thimble and aids in wedging the needle.

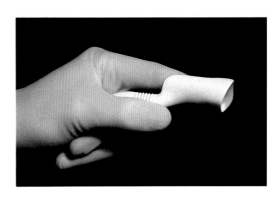

Product **Portable Pacemaker 9790** *pacemaker monitor*
Manufacturer **Medtronic**
Design firm **IDEO Product Development**
Designers **Jochen Backs, Jane Fulton Suri, Bill Verplank**

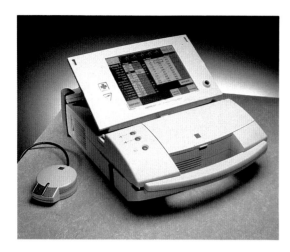

The portability of this system, which checks and adjusts implanted pace-makers, was an essential design criterion. The clever component layout reduces size and increases efficiency in operating procedures. Other design improvements include simplified storage of the cables and other accessories, which may remain plugged in, provision of a writing surface, and a flat paper printer.

Product **System 97 Intra Aortic Balloon Pump**
Manufacturer **Datascope Corporation**
Design firm **Datascope Corporate Design**
Designers **Nicholas Barker, Ken Jones, Rick Reveal**

The sizes of the pump module, the monitor module, and the cart of this equipment were reduced for portability and for ease of use in confined locations, such as helicopters. Self-skinning urethane provides a rugged exterior coating as well as a surface that is soft and warm to the touch. The use of "friendly" colors and shapes brings a soothing element to a serious setting.

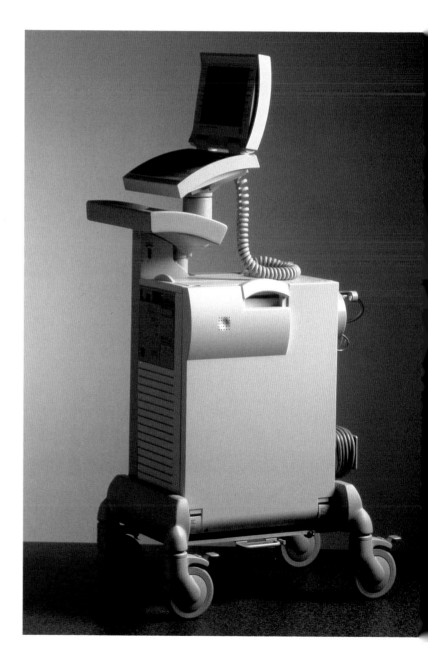

Product Imagn 2000 *diagnostic blood analyzer for HIV positive patients*

Manufacturer Biometric Imaging Inc.

Design firm Lunar Design

Designers Ken Wood, Yves Behar, Rachel Pydrol, Chris Cavell (Lunar Design) Bruno Richet (Function Engineering)

Designed for use in physicians' offices as well as in laboratories, the concept for this product focuses on patient comfort. The interaction areas are well communicated through their design: the front door opens for placement of test cartridges and the oval-shaped well signals the deposit site for the patient's blood sample.

Product Radiology Dictation/Transcription Desktop *(concept)*

Manufacturer Dictaphone Corporation

Design firm Dictaphone Industrial Design Group

Designers David A. Demar, Thomas J. Pendleton

The dictation/transcription desktop addresses the needs of a specific market with an aesthetic that is adaptable to future products. Careful consideration was given to the environment in which the product is used, including lighting conditions, noise levels, and type and frequency of use. Injection-molded ABS with minimal finish application and snap-together parts without fasteners encourages recycling and reuse of components. All electronics are integrated into modules that can be removed and upgraded to extend product life.

Product Opti Pen *semiautomatic insulin injection device*

Manufacturer Hoechst AG

Design group Braun Design Department

Designers Dieter Rams, Jurgen Greubel, Peter Schneider

The design approach here is functional, efficient, and straightforward. It avoids unnecessary embellishment and delivers a simple elegance that communicates clinical quality. This product, with its streamlined design and reduced size, fits like a pen in any pocket or purse.

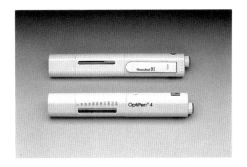

Product BioCAP Workstation *liquid chromatography instrument*

Manufacturer PerSeptive Biosystems

Design firm Design Continuum Inc.

Designers Luis Pedraza, Jopse Tadeo de Castro

For this laboratory instrument, testing processes that normally require five instruments are bundled, while frequently used components are located in one highly accessible area. The design conceals infrequently used components behind closed doors.

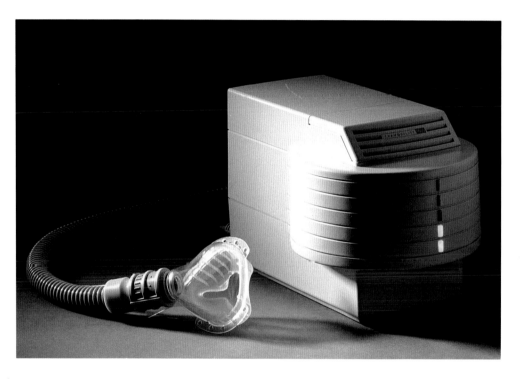

Product Tranquility MP-r *continuous positive air pressure device*

Manufacturer Healthdyne Technologies

Design firm BOLT (formerly Machen Montague)

Designers Dennis Hugley, Wendell Wilson, John Snow, Edgar Montague

The Tranquility is an improved product that assists people with sleeping disorders by providing a controlled air stream into the nose or mouth. Its reduced size allows setup on a bed table, while controls equipped with tactile switch differentiation make the product unique. The elegant form is accentuated by a ribbed circular shape containing the blower, suggesting a metaphorical bellows.

Product Access *immunoassay system*

Manufacturer Sanofi Diagnostics Pasteur

Design firm Design Continuum Inc.

Designers Luis Pedraza, Lynn Noble

The key to this design is simplicity, complementing the analyzer's technical sophistication. The streamlined mechanical layout, a unique carousel design, compactness, and attention to ergonomic detail ensure that every major system resource and device is easily accessible.

Product Checkmate Plus *blood glucose monitoring system*

Manufacturer Cascade Medical

Design firm Worrell Design Inc.

Designer Doug Duchon

Auto-calibration for accurate results, a user-friendly, six-language display that provides words for guidance, a built-in lancing device optimized for minimal pain, and a memory capable of storing 255 test results, characterize this glucose monitoring system.

Product **Finnpipette Bio Control** *multichannel pipette*

Manufacturer **Labsystems OY**

Design firm **E & D Design OY**

Designers **Matti Makkonen, Ari-Pekka Toykkala**

"Natural" finger- and thumb-trigger movements combine the feel and action of manual operation with electronically assisted pipetting. An easy-to-read digital display ensures accurate operation.

Product **Total Knee Replacement Tool**

Manufacturer **Johnson + Johnson**

Design firm **Design Continuum Inc.**

Designers **Stephen Guerra, Jack Gundlach, Greg Hunter**

With extensive task analysis, the design team was able to better understand the existing bone-cutting procedure and how it could be improved. Success rate of the surgery was improved with this new design, which combines the ruggedness needed to cut bone with the precision required in the delicate surgery. To ensure a flat cut at the correct depth, an innovative "captured" slot was developed to allow the surgeon to secure the blade in one direction, while cutting through the patella. The precise depth of the cut is achieved by rotating the knob on top, which adjusts the two prongs under the jaws.

Product **Personal Centrifuge** *fluid separator*
Manufacturer **Denver Instrument**
Design firm **Design Continuum Inc.**
Designers **Luis Pedraza, Noelle Dye (Design Continuum) Mitch Houston, Howard Cano (Denver Instrument)**

This design for a low-cost personal centrifuge offers easy use for multiple tasks, ranging from DNA research to blood testing. The product operates quietly, is small enough to be placed on a desk, protects the fluids and technicians from leaks and spills, and offers clear, immediately understood icons.

Product **Urtemp ME 002** *urine diagnostic device*
Manufacturer **Franklin Diagnostics**
Design firm **Priority Designs**
Designers **Paul Kolada, Vince Haley**

This body-temperature monitoring kit gives a more accurate reading by measuring urine temperature. The design is simple and reliable.

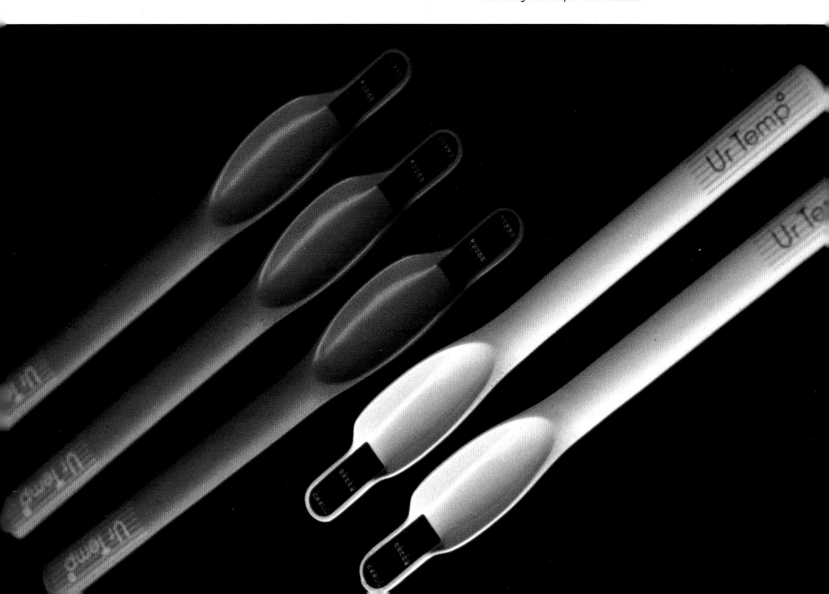

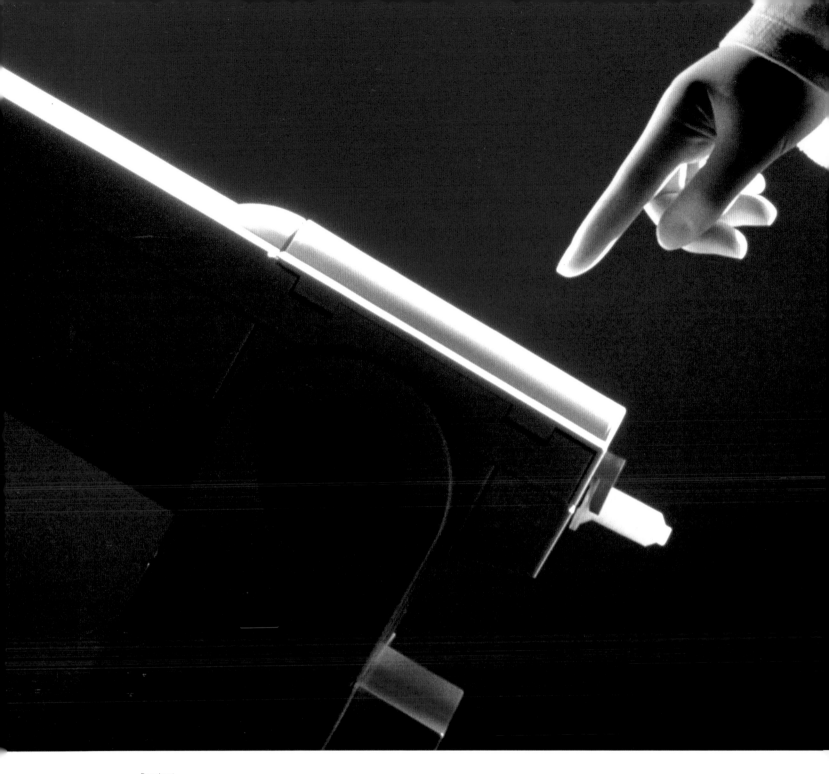

Product	Pentamix *dental mixing unit*
Manufacturer	ESPE
Design firm	Neumeister Design
Designer	Alexander Neumeister

The Pentamix Polether mixing system is used for dental practices. Within a few seconds it supplies absolutely homogenous polyether impression material. A clear cut classic design that is ergonomic in design and reliable in function.

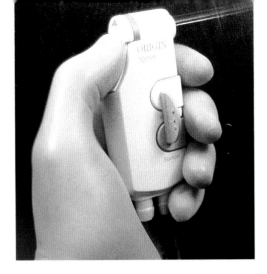

Product   Suction Irrigation Device

Manufacturer Origin MedSystems, MedTech Group

Design firm Steiner Design Associates and Synectic Engineering

Designers   Mark Steiner, Jeff Stein, John Harrison, Allan Bachman
             (Steiner Design Associates), Rich Mueller, Jay Watkins,
             Joseph Mandato (MedTech Group)

The instrument is a disposable device used to irrigate bleed-
ing tissues and to suction excess fluids from the surgical
area in non-invasive laprascopic surgery. The device is
reduced in size, while the large button control provides easy
activation. The raised rib protruding from the button offers
tactile recognition and prevents the surgeon's finger from
sliding down the instrument. A second instrument can also
be inserted though the back of this product.

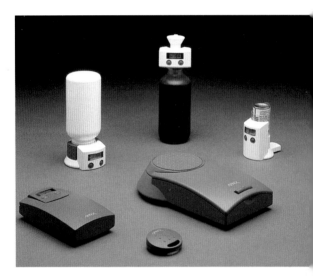

Product   Mems® Medication Management System

Manufacturer Aprex Corporation

Design firm IDEO Product Development

Designers   Jochen Backs, Doug Satzger

This monitoring system is designed to help patients
remember their medication. The standard cap on a
patient's drug container is replaced with the Mems
system, which then electronically records the time
and date each time the patient opens the container.
An electronic reader transfers the data to a
personal computer.

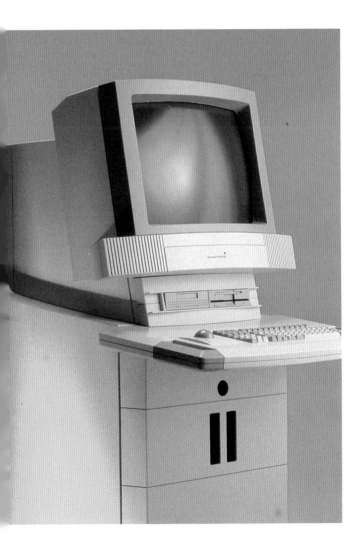

Product   Sonic CT *breast imaging system*

Manufacturer ThermoTrex Corporation

Design firm ROGOV International Design

Designer   Vladymir Rogov

The Sonic CT is a breast imaging system for the early diagnosis of breast cancer. Low-frequency sound waves and com-
puted tomography provide crisply defined images of breast
tissue without ionizing radiation or painful body compression.

NEW TOOLS

A good tool is a respected object often serving a long and useful life, and in some cases handed down over the years. While many of today's tools are electronic, there is an even greater requirement for ergonomics and ease of use. This is reflected in the design briefs of most of these products. Many of the products shown require a good hand, eye, or ear to use them, thus the human factor is of primary importance in the design of these New Tools.

5

Product	Hand Axe
Manufacturer	Fiskars OY AB
Design firm	Fiskars Design
Designers	Svante Ronnhîlm, Olavi Linden, Kenneth Wickstrîm

The Finnish firm Fiskars has been making axes since the seventeenth century and for this product they looked back 100,000 years to the stone age axe. The axe head sits inside the plastic handle, which was traditionally designed and shaped for a firm chopping grip. The combined blade guard and carrying handle is a very safe and practical solution to cutting dangers.

Product · Olympus BX Series Microscope
Manufacturer · Olympus Optical Co., Ltd.
Design firm · frogdesign inc.
Designer · team frogdesign

The ergonomic design of this micro-scope increases operation comfort, and fatigue-free observation. Electrical components are located in the back to allow workspace on the left and right of the stand. This product is eyepoint height for comfortable observation.

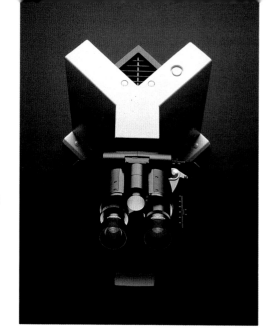

Product · DCT-700 *recording equipment*
Manufacturer · Ampex Corp.
Design firm · Ampex Corporate Industrial Design
Designers · Darrell Staley, Ron Boeder

This is a state-of-the-art family of products for broadcast recording, switching, and special effects for video. Grouped together for easy-to-reach controls, this line presents a strong and consistent visual image for the company.

Product Tapemate *calculator*

Manufacturer Digitool Corporation

Design firm River Studio

Designers William Lipsey, David Gresham, Richard Bates

The Tapemate clips onto a standard tape rule and calculates in the foot/inch/fraction system. It measures areas and volumes automatically. Solar-powered in a rugged, dustproof case, this tool is used by designers and handymen alike.

Product PowerShot™ *heavy duty staplegun*

Manufacturer Black & Decker

Design firms Worktools, Inc./Innovations & Development

Designers Joel Marks (Worktools Inc.), Gary Grossman (Innovations & Development)

The PowerShot™ staple gun uses a forward-action design with such ergonomic features as a split-grip rubber-coated handle and a window to indicate when reloading is required. Clean lines and a curved back give the tool a powerful professional appearance.

Product **Color Spectrometer**

Manufacturer **Light Source Inc.**

Design firm **IDEO Product Development**

Designers **Chris Loew, Chris Robinette**

This attractive and efficient color spectrometer can check luminous or pigment color and translate these readings to formulas for various media, making it a valuable, timesaving tool for graphic designers.

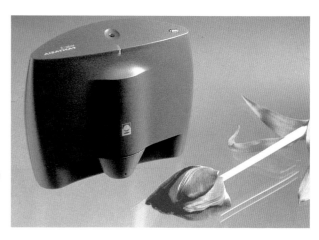

Product **Lumina** *slide illuminator*

Manufacturer **Leaf Systems, Inc.**

Design firm **Product Insight, Inc.**

Designers **Bryan Hotaling, Jon Rossman**

A desktop accessory for the Leaf digital camera, this product illuminates 35mm slides and 57mm transparencies for production-quality digital image creation.

Product   Mechanic's Creeper
Manufacturer   Detailed Designs
Design firm   Michael W. Young Associates
Designers   Michael W. Young, Chig-Ping Hsia, Sheng-Fu Lee, Wei Young

The Creeper is used by auto mechanics to lie on their backs under cars. Based on ergonomic studies, the creeper was designed to follow the contours of the human body, and to support stress areas including the pelvis, lumbar region, thorax, cervical spine, and the head. It has two deep pockets for tools, and handles for carrying.

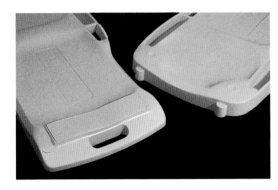

Product   Saw Ingletadora
Manufacturer   Talleres Casals, S.A.
Design firm   Flores Associates
Designer   Antoni Flores

This sleek tablesaw performs all of the required functions in a most elegant way. Its clean, black design provides a refreshing aesthetic, while the compact size and quickly adjustable blades make it less cumbersome than traditional saws, and easier to operate.

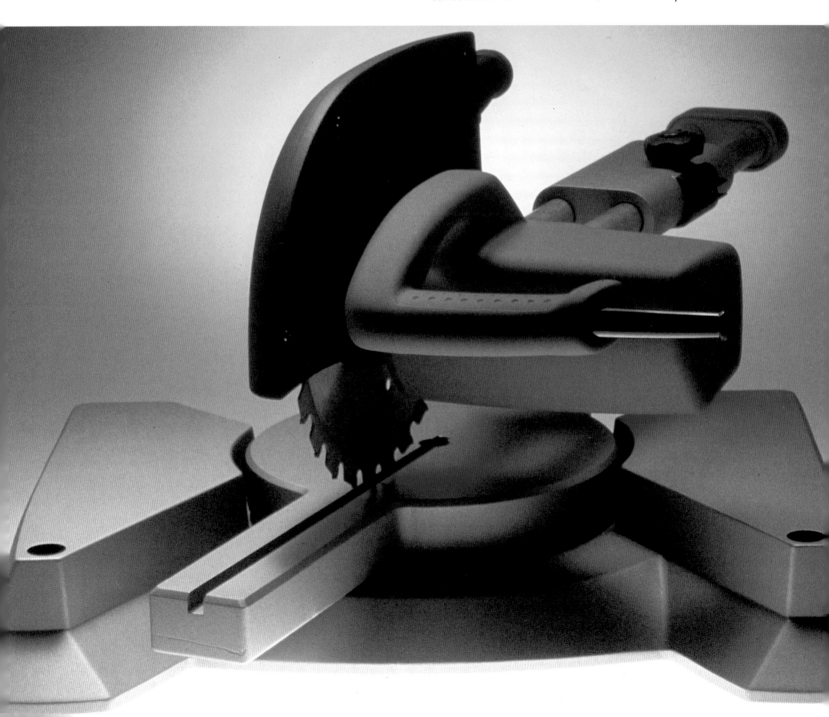

Product   Accumet *pH meter*

Manufacturer   Denver Instruments, Inc.

Design firm   ZIBA Design, Inc

Designers   Sohrab Vossoughi, Christopher Alviar

Used to measure the pH value, tension, temperature, and conductivity of fluids, this product is very user-friendly. Accumet is angled for comfortable viewing and operation, and the keys are domed for easy contact. The rubber surface material is soft to the touch and protects the unit from the rigors of laboratory usage.

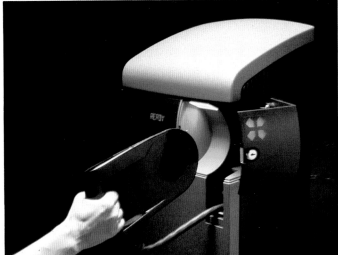

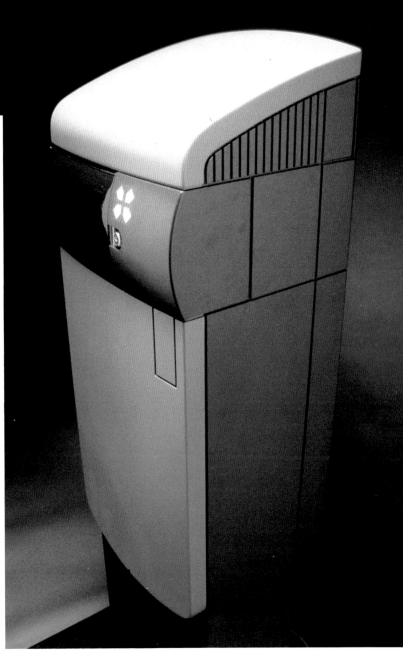

Product Electric Car Charging Station

Manufacturer G.M. Hughes Power Control Systems

Design firm Ciro Design

Designers Richard Jung, Dennis Grudt, Barbara Brodsky (Paddle Design-IDEO)

This product design incorporates security, functionality, and ergonomics. The unit is tamper-proof and weather-resistant, all within a well-designed enclosure.

Product In-Store Display System

Manufacturer Post Inc.

Design firm INTERFORM

Designer Peter H. Müller

This in-store display system is suspended from a hoop and provides computer-graphic customer information in a pre-selectable portrait or landscape format.

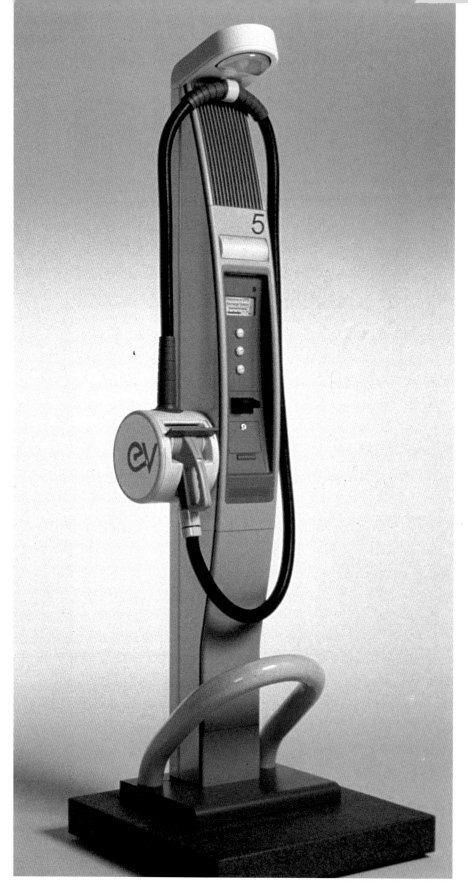

Product Electric Vehicle Recharge Station (concept)

Manufacturer Electric Power Research Institute

Design firm Teague

Designers Jeff Brown, Doug Grambush, Steve Vordenberg, Brad Clarkson

This concept design was created for public-parking facilities, with the goal of developing a cost-effective infrastructure to support electric vehicles. The design builds on the familiarity of self-service gas pumps and automatic-teller machines.

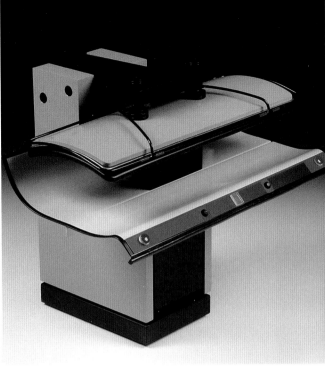

Product Laundry Press and Ironing Press
Manufacturer Pantex Winschoten
Design firm Peter Stut Industrial Design

The laundry and ironing press industry now provides improved product design with better ergonomic/interfacial functioning, faster and more silent operation, and an image based on strong visual and functional elements.

Product Taipei Public Telephone Booth *(concept)*
Designers Dennis Chan, Philip T.K. Lin

The concept was a result of a telephone booth design competition in Taiwan. Telephone booths worldwide seem to have a strong cultural element, this example employs the Ming Dynasty image. The concept is also quite practical with an adjustable phone height for various users.

Product BMW DIS Tester *diagnosis system*

Manufacturer Siemens/BMW

Design firm Neumeister Design

Designer Alexander Neumeister

The compact design and easy-to-read display of this mobile diagnosis system for automobiles reflects the car-maker's high standards of design.

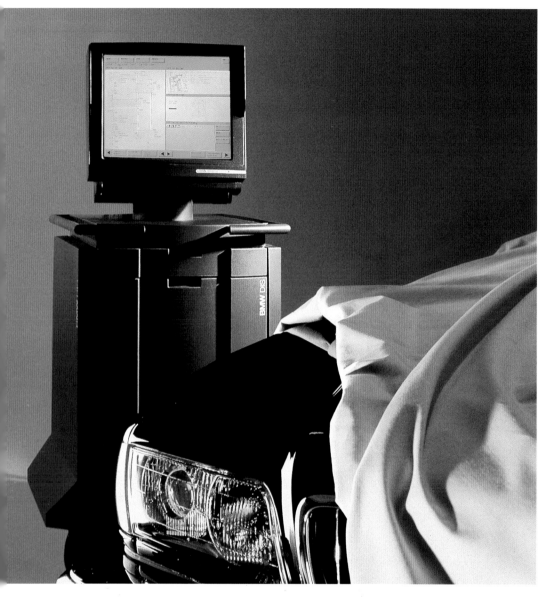

Product Buscom *fare collection system*

Manufacturer Buscom OY

Design firm E & D Design OY

Designers Tapani Hyv nen, Matti Koivisto

In modern mass transit, boarding times are of key importance, and this SMART CARD system has the advantage of speed. Passengers can walk past the reader without stopping, and the card is read from the traveler's hand.

Product **24/48 Dash Tape Recorder**
Manufacturer **Studer AG**
Design firm **VIA 4**

This digital tape recorder is part of a new and unique design language. The ergonomic quality of the cleanly structured machine and remote control gives the unit a special élan.

Product **Inform System** *tourist aid*
Manufacturer **Acoustiguide**
Design firm **ECCO Design Inc.**
Designers **Eric Chan, Jeff Miller**

This personal digital tour guide allows users to access commentaries on any exhibit, in any sequence desired, by entering an identification number on the keypad. It is designed to be easily understood and operated by first-time users, regardless of language or product familiarity.

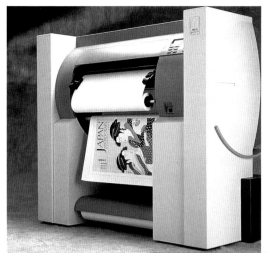

Product **SummaChrome** *color printer*

Manufacturer **Summagraphics**

Design firm **Design Edge**

Designers **Mark S. Kimbrough, IDSA, Randall Decker, IDSA**

This sleek product breaks the big, beige, and box-like tradition of large peripheral printers. The product design communicates the unique mechanical features of the printer and makes its use more convenient by allowing the printing process to be viewed as the color image is created.

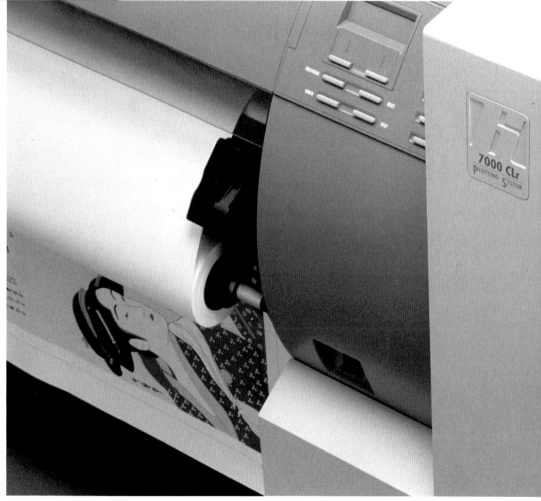

Product **Vicom CRT** *information/communication unit*

Manufacturer **NYNEX Science and Technology Division**

Design firm **ECCO Design, Inc.**

Designers **Eric Chan, Eyal Eliav, Jeff Miller**

With combined telephone, computer, and video technology, Vicom's liquid crystal display delivers diverse and sophisticated functions in a compact, user-friendly device. The product features an on-line data bank, voice and data message storage and playback, and an interactive screen.

Product Geoblade™
Manufacturer Rollerblade, Inc.
Design firm Design Continuum Inc.
Designers Michel Arney, Carl Madore

With this model, the designers created the first of an entirely new skate series which includes a range of new skates—each with a distinctive look—and uses the same component, the bottom of the skate. Although a greater initial investment in tooling, the approach allows the bottom portion of the skate to be successfully leveraged over a full product line, offering greater economies over time.

The Velcro strap, single buckle and mid entry design make it very quick and easy to slip into the skate, characteristics which appeal to the recreational skater (the target market for the Geoblade). In addition, the strap offers a good fit without the problems associated with laces or the bulkiness and vulnerability of buckles. The skate offers an integrated ventilation strategy and a sleek, aerodynamic appeal, an important feature to fashion-conscious skaters.

Some of today's freshest product design ideas can be found in the design of recreational and sports equipment. Designed for high performance in competitive situations, sports equipment must not only be ergonomic, but must meet rigorous safety standards as well. Apart from these essential considerations, sports equipment offers fertile ground for designers to express imagery that reflects the connection of the human body and spirit with the "tools" that enable physical action, whether it is at a leisurely or demanding level.

Product HR 2000 *heart rate monitor*

Manufacturer Vetta Sports (Orleander Group)

Design firm Tres Design Group, Inc.

Designers Francois Geneve, Luc Heiligenstein,
Stephen Melamed, & Peter Langmar

This heart rate monitor and computer
designed for sports training fits easily on
the wrist and is lightweight and waterproof.

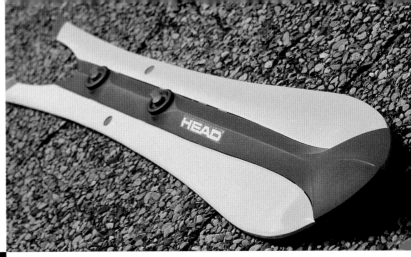

Product See-Lecta *combination ski/snowboard*

Manufacturer Head AG

Designer Satyendra Pakhale

The See-Lecta offers the user a combination snowboarding/ski experience. A new binding design, Universal Binding, and an injection-molded interior and shell exterior make it possible to join two skis together to form a snow board.

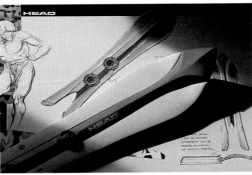

Product Lifestride 5500™ *consumer treadmill*

Manufacturer Life Fitness, Inc.

Design firm Cesaroni Design Associates, Inc.

Designer Steve Doehler

A combination of materials and design makes this exercise equipment compatible with residential interior settings. The user-friendly handlebar area is compression-molded fiberglass. Visually, the handlebars make a smooth transition into the soft contours of the console and vertical support tubes. The sculptural accessory trays hold paraphernalia such as a water bottle, cordless phone, or personal stereo.

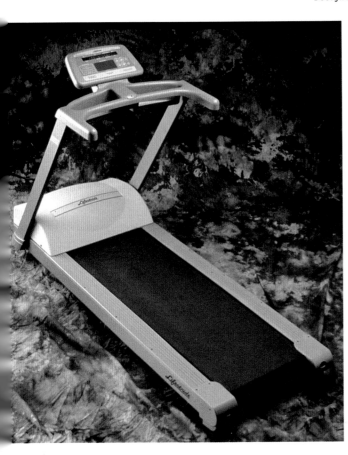

Product **CupBall** *game*

Design firm **The Axis Group Inc.**

Designer **Alexander Manu**

CupBall is a game of skill that can be played by one or more players. The concept was inspired by "cup and ball," a traditional toy in many cultures. This modern version of the game is designed to have universal appeal.

Product **Basketball Stat Pro** *calculator*

Manufacturer **Vertical Product Development**

Design firm **Taylor & Chu**

Designer **Neil Taylor**

The basketball-statistic calculator automates the collection and calculation of individual player and team statistics. The grid and controls can be quickly accessed, allowing users to keep up with the fast-paced games, and the large elastomeric keys are separated into common functionality groups for ease of use.

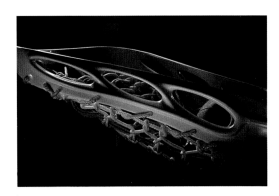

Product **Lacrosse Stick Head**
Manufacturer **STX**
Design firm **Priority Designs**
Designers **Paul Kolada, Terry Birchler**

This lacrosse stick uses injection-molded plastic in place of the traditional wood and leather materials, giving the stick a low wall and a light feel.

Product **ELB Fitness Ergometer E 420**
Manufacturer **Tunturipyota OY**
Design firm **E & D Design OY**
Designers **Heikki Kiiski, Jouni Teittinen**

The sinuous organic form makes this exercise machine easy to use, while the coloration of the base invites approach.

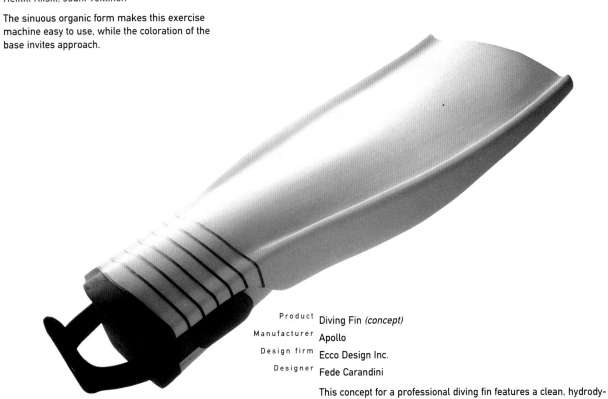

Product **Diving Fin** *(concept)*
Manufacturer **Apollo**
Design firm **Ecco Design Inc.**
Designer **Fede Carandini**

This concept for a professional diving fin features a clean, hydrodynamic form a fast release, and a fast adjustment-strap mechanism.

Product   Swing Finder Muscle Memory Tutor *golf instructional device*

Manufacturer   Felicity Services

Design firm   Priority Designs

Designers   Paul Kolada, Vince Haley

This product was designed to aid the novice golfer in developing and maintaining a proper golf stroke by emphasizing a turning rather than a swaying movement in the stroke. A large viewing mirror (complete with an oval, parallax hole that creates a third dimension), a liquid bubble-level to balance the product on most terrains, and an adjustable lid make this product unique.

Product High-performance Protective Gear *in-line skating gear*
Manufacture Rollerblade, Inc.
Design firm Metaphase Design Group, Inc.
Designers/Researchers Bryce G. Rutter, Ph.D., Douglas Miller, Michael Austrin,
John Loudenslager (Metaphase) Jamie Kalvestran,
Tim Weiner (Rollerblade)

A design research study, which investigated existing protection techniques, relevant ergonomic issues, varying size requirements, and experience with in-line injuries, helped Rollerblade to identify and understand in-line skating injuries to the wrist, knee, and elbow. The resulting protective-gear designs improve both injury prevention, with stronger, more cushioned materials at impact points, and wearer comfort, with more flexible material placed at inside joint areas.

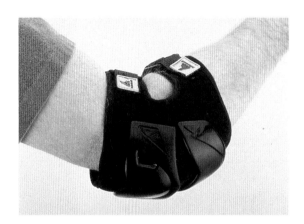

Product Cycling Helmet
Manufacturer Giro Sports
Design firm Design Continuum, Inc.
Designers Michel Arney, Ed Chalmers (Giro), Bob Lakes (Giro)

This is the first bike helmet designed to remain in a stable and proper head position throughout the rigors of mountain biking. The design offers a lightly sprung support system against the lower region of the head. It has sufficient flex for the user to slip it on, yet remains firmly but lightly in place. Stretch fabrics prevent uncomfortable heat buildup. Safety as well as comfort were the key objectives of the project.

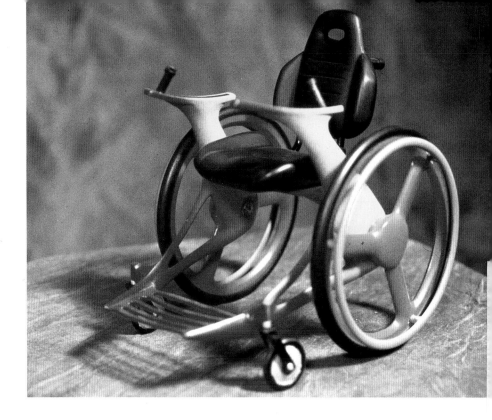

Product Meteor *youth sports wheelchair*

Designer Anthony D. Shoemaker

This wheelchair turns attention to a new area of design exploration.

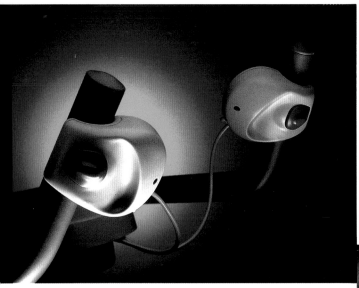

Product Exertainment™ *interactive fitness system*

Manufacturer Life Fitness, Inc.

Design firm Cesaroni Design Associates, Inc.

Designers Jason Alvarez, Dan Gremonprez

Ergonomic left and right controllers clip to the handlebars of this exercise equipment, allowing the exerciser to play a Super Nintendo video game while working out. The game screen also displays a progress report on the level of exercise.

Product Scorpio *wheel straightener*

Manufacturer Technische Industrie Tacx BV

Design firm Ninaber/Peters/Krouwel Industrial Design

Designer Peter Krouwel

This folding device uses red sensors to alert bikers to lateral and radial defects in their wheel rims positioned close to the bicycle's wheels. The tool is elegant in both form and function, a characteristic emphasized by its sleek red, black, and metal-toned colors.

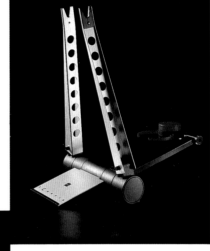

Product Cyclestand *bicycle stand*

Manufacturer Technische Industrie Tacx BV

Design firm Ninaber/Peters/Krouwel Industrial Design

Designer Peter Krouwel

The task of repairing and servicing bicycle tires is aided with more ergonomically correct positioning, which is made possible by this stand.

Product **Night Mariner** *scope*

Manufacturer ITT

Design firm BOLT (formerly Machen Montague)

Designers Mark Gildersleeve, Dennis Huguley,
Bob Gibson, Edgar Montague

This design translates night-vision
defense technology into a new scope
for the commercial marine market. All
adjustments are controlled by tactile
recognition. Its lightweight and compact
size make it easily portable.

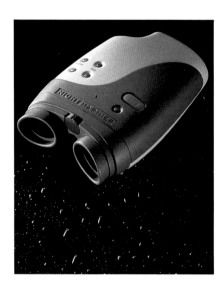

Product Berkley New Generation Fishing Reels

Manufacturer Berkley

Design firm IDEO Product Development

Designers Mark Biasotti, Chris Robinette

This family of reels includes everything the first-time fisher-
man needs to get started. The ergonomic, energetic design
has fewer parts to master, making these ensembles attractive
to beginners of any age.

Product The Natural Hatch System & Fly Box

Manufacturer Woods & Brooks

Design group Woods & Brooks

Designers John Stribiak, Tom Noone, Dave Plahm, Bruce Andre

A system of removable fly trays permits the user to carry only those trays appropriate for the day's outing.

Product The Natural Hatch Tying System

Manufacturer Woods & Brooks

Design group Woods & Brooks

Designers John Stribiak, Tom Noone, Dave Plahm, Bruce Andre

The compact functionality of this mahogany box is updated with exterior convenience features, and designed for portability.

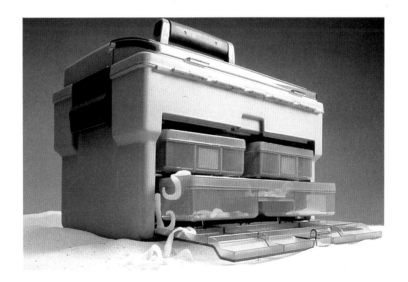

Product Pro Series Fishing and Tackle Boxes

Manufacturer Rubbermaid

Design firm Design Central

Designers John Koenig, Jeff DeBord, Hank Kahl (Rubbermaid)

Rainer Teufel, Diana Juratovac (Design Central)

Flexible internal storage containers allow users to customize these tackle boxes. Two-way access permits easy entry to top bins, while sport grips hold lures firmly in place.

INFORMATION 7

The conceptual projects in this section, such as the Electronic Groupware Table, Explorations of the Qualities of the New Office Landscape, the Soft Notebook Computer, and the Epcot Center Innoventions exhibit suggest how information tools might look in the next millennium, if not sooner.

There is a refreshing trend toward greater freedom of form in information product design. Efforts to depart from the stereotypical, look-alike equipment that has dominated this industry for the past decade abound, not only to differentiate products from those of competitors, but as earnest attempts to reduce their intimidating character for users. In this context, top-notch ergonomic aspects of the equipment are a given; designers are focusing on the semantic qualities of their products in order to achieve both differentiation and a more felicitous relationship with both the user and the surrounding environment.

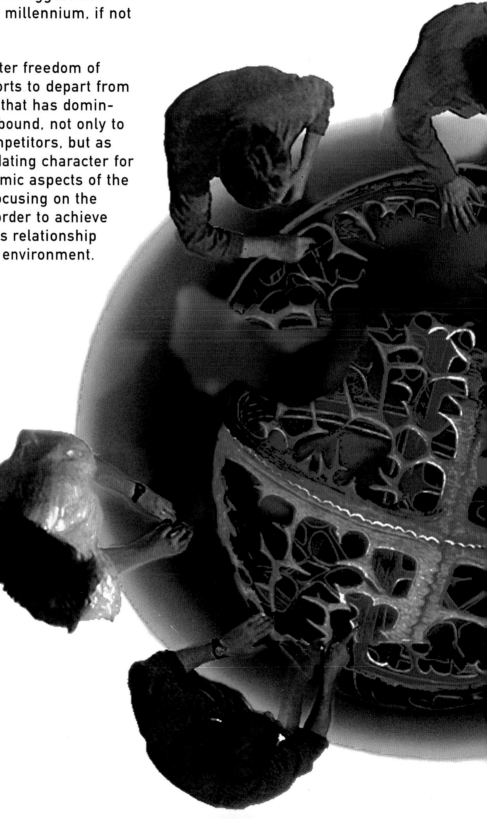

Product Electronic Groupware Table *work area (concept)*

Design firm Fahnstrom/McCoy

Designers Michael McCoy, Denise Heckman

Predictions for the future of electronic worktools suggest that groups of people will come together to do interactive, non-hierarchical work. At the Groupware Table, participants use hand gestures as well as pens and cursor controls to manipulate information. Images are gathered and juxtaposed in a fluid and communal way on the multiple nodes of touch-sensitive displays and work surfaces. Subgroups can leave and rejoin the main group as the project evolves. Digital communications technology allows information to be shared simultaneously with groups in other locations, joining people in a common task.

Product **Pentium** *notebook computer*
Manufacturer **IBM**
Design firm **Design Edge**
Designers **Mark Kimbrough, IDSA, Greg Hinzmann, IDSA**

The Pentium notebook computer appeals to both the aesthetic sensibilities and the technology requirements of the business executive. It offers the latest color LCD technology and features built-in stereo speakers for multimedia applications. The TrackPoint@ cursor control embedded in the keyboard replaces the conventional mouse for point-and-click operations. An innovative, contoured palm rest and latches-and-button design speak to the concern for ergonomics. The muted green color is a departure from the traditional charcoal or beige, giving the computer an unconventional, yet elegant personality.

Product **VR 2000** *computer system*
Manufacturer **SDI Virtual Reality Corporation**
Design firm **The Axis Group Inc.**
Designer **Alexander Manu**

The VR 2000 generates photo-realistic, high definition 3-D images on a surround screen. The triangular geometry of the housing takes into account the computer's primary application—use in specially designed rooms in attraction parks. Designed for flexibility, the computer can be arranged in configurations of up to eight stacked units.

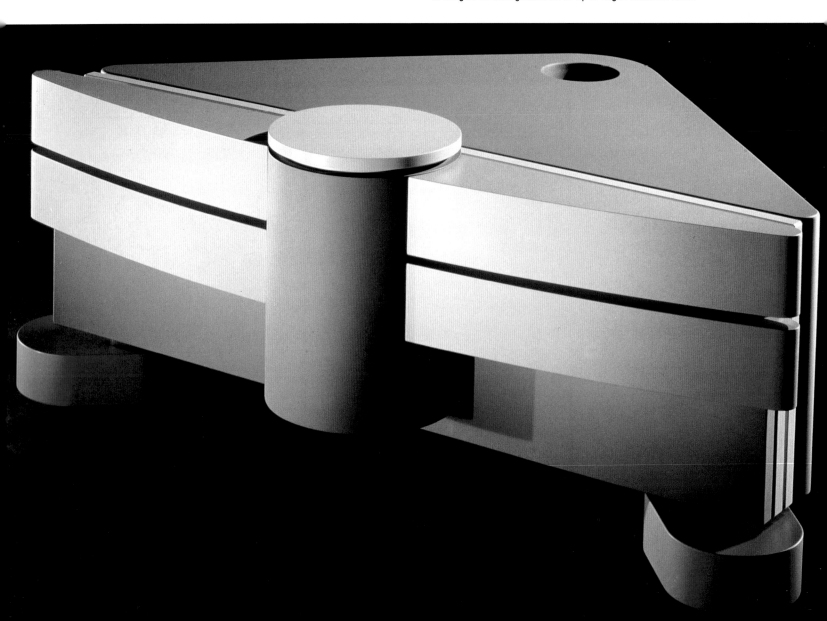

Product Trackball

Manufacturer Dexixa

Design firm Montgomery Pfeiffer

This trackball is an ergonomic static
pointing device. Its asymmetrical ball
and contoured buttons were designed
to reduce exertion and muscle stress.
It also requires a minimum of desktop space.

Product Videoman *computer video camera*

Manufacturer Logitech

Design firm Montgomery Pfeiffer

This is a color digital-video camera for real-
time conferences and production of video
clips. The camera's arm is extendible and the
head can be detached from its base and
placed on top of the monitor. The video head
rotates from a portrait mode to a document-
imaging mode.

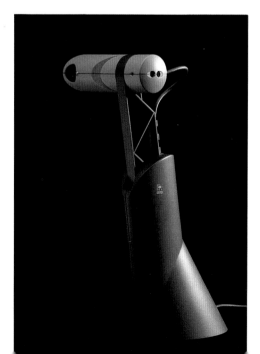

Product   Manta *monitor*

Manufacturer   Hewlett Packard

Design firm   ZIBA Design Inc.

Designers   Sohrab Vossoughi, Jan Hippen, Henry Chin

The design challenge was to create an innovative and visually distinctive work-station monitor for financial institutions. This product is approachable due to its visual form. The open arms of the base face the user and the gently arced support arm presents the screen. The product's sculptural quality contributes to the total atmosphere of the work environment.

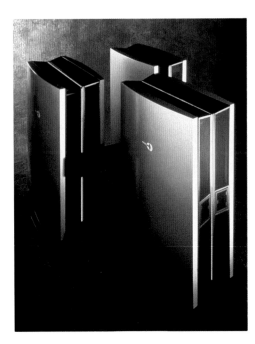

Product   Exemplar Supercomputer

Manufacturer   Convex

Design firm   frogdesign inc.

Designers   team frogdesign

This system is easily expandable from one to eight towers. The light display consists of a thin band of lights that wraps up the front of the tower, across the top and down the back, optimizing visibility. The towers are arranged in a staggered configuration in consideration of space planning and ergonomics.

Product   Soft Notebook Computer *(concept)*

Design firm   Emilio Ambasz & Associates Inc.

Designer   Emilio Ambasz

The traditional paper notebook inspired the design of this user-friendly notebook computer. The usual hard shell exterior gives way to foam-padded leather, which opens to reveal a soft, tactile, rubber keypad and thin LCD display. The screen can be adjusted, like an easel, with a Velcro tab. Opening the unit reveals storage for diskettes, pockets for paper and business cards, and a pen for using the computer as an electronic sketch pad.

Product   Concept Computers/Epcot Center Innoventions Exhibit *(concept)*

Manufacturer   Apple Computer

Design firm   Lunar Design

Design team   David Laituri (Lunar Design), Robert Brunner (Apple)

These two conceptual products for home office and kitchen were developed for the Innoventions Exhibit at Disneyworld's Epcot Center. The kitchen computer includes touchscreen interface, built-in imaging system and camera for video messaging, and controls compatible with total home automation of utilities and functions such as gas, water, and light. The home office model, a keyboardless computer controlled by a wireless pen and pad input device, combines plastic parts with wooden accents. This computer is an integrated printer/scanner and has video-conferencing ability and a cordless phone.

Product   Joule Drive *disk drive*

Manufacturer   LaCie, Ltd.

Design firm   ZIBA Design, Inc.

Designers   Sohrab Vossoughi, Mark Stella

The Joule Drive is a flexible disk-array system for Macintosh computers. The product's vertical configuration visually differentiates it from conventional mass storage products. The design echoes the plug-and-play ease of use, and the compact footprint enables users to build high-capacity desktop systems quickly and easily. The drive's deep green color and purple accents stand out against less colorful competitors.

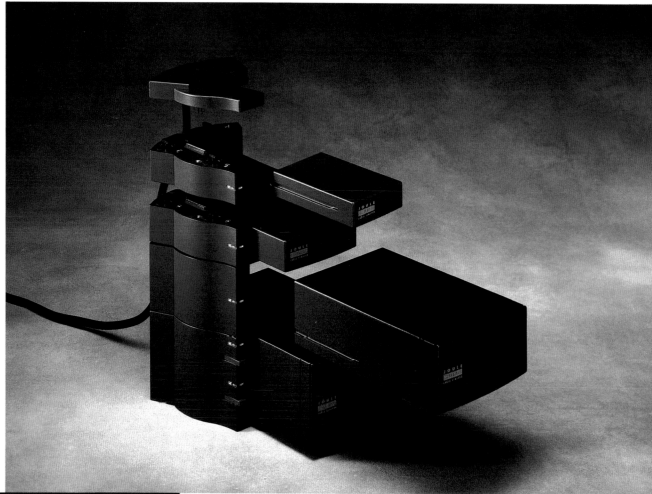

Product	Color LCD Monitor
Manufacturer	Chicony Electronics
Design firm	Design Edge
Designers	Mark Kimbrough, Greg Hinzmann

This versatile desk-top or wall-mounted monitor incorporates a color LCD screen, built-in speakers, and a microphone. An optional touch screen is available for wall-mounted use, such as public information monitors. The screen adjusts vertically and can be tilted out to optimize the viewing angle.

Product	Joystick
Manufacturer	Dexixa
Design firm	Montgomery Pfeiffer

Joystick features a "soft" handle with wraparound finger grips and two integrated trigger buttons. The design allows for good control and fast movement with a minimum of user fatigue. A profiled base supports the palm of the hand.

Product   Digital Connexions *desktop voice processor*

Manufacturer   Dictaphone Corporation

Design firm   Dictaphone Industrial Design Group

Designers   Sandor Weisz, David Demar, Thomas Pendleton

The product features two dictation voice-input devices, including a hand microphone and a handset with controls. A large, hinged LCD screen is adjustable to different viewing angles, and the soft keycaps are sculpted for comfort.

Product   Audiovision 5.5m Display *computer monitor*

Manufacturer   Apple Computer, Inc.

Design firm   IDEO Product Development/Apple Computer, Inc.

Designers   Mark Biasotti, Ricardo Salinas, Chris Hosking (IDEO), Raymond Riley, Robert Brunner, Dave Lundgren (Apple Computer, Inc.)

Audio and video features are effectively integrated into the design of this computer monitor. The acoustic chamber in the bottom of the monitor gives excellent sound reproduction, while the total design is a refreshing change from the standard monitor aesthetic.

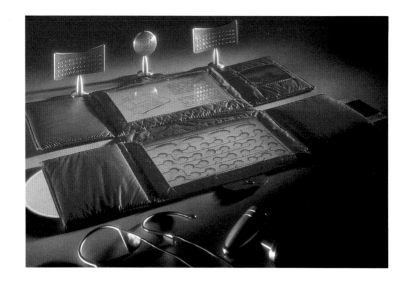

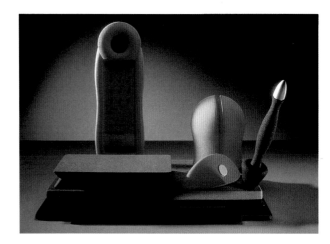

Product : Exploration of the Qualities of the New Office Landscape

design workshop (concept)

Design firm : Philips Corporate Design; Olivetti Design Division

Concepts for future products are developed in workshops, then shown to customers, press, opinion leaders, and the general public for feedback. The Magic Carpet *(top)* is a soft, portable desktop which unrolls and provides a working environment with a CD-ROM, electronic tablet, speakers, and accessories. The Communicator *(middle)* is a desktop landscape with tablet, mouse, and speakers. The Portrait *(bottom)* is a small, transparent notebook that opens like a journal and is connected to an electronic placemat containing peripherals for printing and messaging.

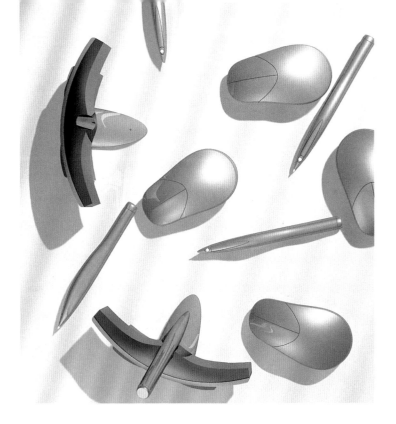

Product
Freepoint Aero Duet *wireless input system*

Manufacturer
Creative Technology

Design firm
Ginko Design, Inc.

Designers
Scott S.H.Yu, Irene Chen-Jones, Sean Ro

Freepoint Aero Duet meets the challenge of combining mouse, pen, and digitizer into an ergonomic infrared input system. Patented wireless infrared technology enables free movement in a 3-D virtual workspace. The receiver tracks the movements of the device and sends the data to the host PC.

Product
"Nature" Contour Keyboard

Manufacturer
Microsoft Corporation

Design firm
ZIBA Design

Designers
Sohrab Vossoughi, Jan Hippen, Penny Yao

This is an approachable, ergonomically correct keyboard. The Contour is easy to use with no complicated adjustments to make or attachments to assemble. To simplify use, the split angle of the Contour is fixed, and to enhance comfort, the surface of the keyboard is gently peaked at the center.

Product PoquetPad *personal digital assistant*

Manufacturer Fujitsu

Design firm Taylor & Chu

Designer Robin Chu

Weighing in at a little over a pound and with a footprint half the size of traditional field-automation systems, the PoquetPad balances requirements of long battery life and large LCD with the need for small size and weight.

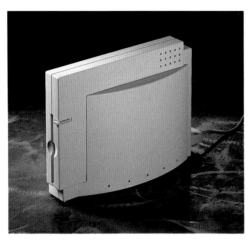

Product LAN Micro Tower

Manufacturer NCR Corporation

Design firm ZIBA Design, Inc.

Designers Sohrab Vossoughi, Christopher Alviar

The LAN Micro Tower's pure form simplifies the workstation environment with its compactness and calm presence. By placing a workstation on a desktop or shelf, the computer's power is always within easy reach. The design is user-friendly, and its clean form and compact size enable it to transcend technology and become a personal tool.

Product Cricket 3-D *input device*

Manufacturer Digital Image Design

Design firm ECCO Design Inc.

Designers Eric Chan, Jeff Miller, Eyal Eliav

In the sophisticated, 3-D computer world, the power of the computer is often limited by its inputting device. The Cricket was designed to dramatically outperform existing 3-D mouse products and other 3-D interaction tools. The Cricket features an ergonomic grip, multiple input controls, and tactile feedback.

Product Personal Visual Communication System

Manufacturer PictureTel Corporation

Design firm Design Continuum Inc.

Designers John Costello, Michel Arney, Benjamin Beck, Richard Leiterman

In work environments already crowded with electronic and other office equipment, the challenge is to integrate high quality teleconferencing equipment as unobtrusively as possible. This system accomplishes the goal with compact, versatile, dual-purpose components that are easy to set up and operate.

Product Modular Computer

Manufacturer Motorola Computer Group

Design firm Palo Alto Design Group Inc.

Designers Thomas Shoda, Ted Santos, John Toor

The Motorola modular computer integrates the concept of modularity and ease of use in the powerful VME computing system. Designed for stand-alone or rack-mounted installations, the modular bezels and internal components can be arranged and configured to the user's needs.

Product **Notebook Computer**

Manufacturer **Chicony Electronics**

Design firm **New Product Design**

Designers **Gene Yanky, Ron Boeder, Phil Frank**

This product's unique package combines the traditional notebook functions with a pen-based application. It can be used as both a portable notebook with full-function keyboard, or as a handheld pad.

Product Scanman Easytouch *scanner*
Manufacturer Logotech
Design firm Montgomery Pfeiffer

The Scanman is a small device for gray-scale scanning. The sloped shape provides a firm grip and directional tracking, and the product is lightweight and portable.

Product Ellipstone *mouse*
Manufacturer Elecom Corporation
Design firm ZIBA Design, Inc.
Designers Sohrab Vossoughi, Hiro Watanabe

The use of this mouse is highly intuitive. The keys are placed at different heights, so the user need not look at the mouse during use. Hand comfort was a primary objective of the design. By creating an undercut, the fingers can fit comfortably underneath the product making it easy to lift and move the mouse. It is analagous to holding a soft stone in your hand.

Product	LAN Keystation
Manufacturer	NCR Corporation
Design firm	ZIBA Design
Designers	Sohrab Vossoughi, Christopher Alviar

The LAN Keystation is a fully featured, high-performance workstation embedded in a full-sized keyboard. It has a high-touch, high adaptability approach to the ergonomics of PC workstations. Clearing the CPU off the desktop and integrating it within the keyboard places all the controls at the user's fingertips. The LAN Keystation gives users the power to control both their desk tops and their computing capability.

Product	AS/400 Advanced Series
Manufacturer	IBM
Design firm	IBM
Designers	David Hill, Tim Murphy
Photography	Bill Diers, Greer and Assoc.

The industrial design objective was to reinvent a visual identity for the AS/400 Advanced Series. The five new product enclosures feature cylindrical rear covers, innovative keys, integrated control panel protection, and deep, penetrating air inlets, all in a unifying black color.

Product SunFax 100 *facsimile machine*
Manufacturer Vidar SMS
Design firm The Axis Group Inc.
Designers Alexander Manu

The SunFax 100 is an unobstrusive piece of equipment with a pure, recognizable, geometric shape.
The multilayered appearance identifies the controls,
displays, and paper rolls.

Product Adjustable Keyboard System
Manufacturer Apple Computer Inc.
Design firm Apple Computer, Vent Design
Designers David Shen, Ray Riley(Apple), Stephen Peart,
Eric Chin(Vent Design)

This is a highly flexible, full-function keyboard.
The inclusion of palm rests, which attach to the
"split" keycap groups, allows for a neutral limb
position. The separate, extended keypad can be
placed to the left or right of the keyboard. All of
these features make this a truly ergonomic
solution.

Product MultiSpin 3Xp *portable CD-ROM reader*
Manufacturer NEC
Design firm Fahnstrom/McCoy
Designers Dale Fahnstrom, Michael McCoy, Davis Van den
Branden, Scott Ternovits

The MultiSpin 3Xp is a high-performance,
triple-speed portable computer ROM and
audio disk-reader for all DOS, Windows, and
Macintosh platforms. The aesthetic character
of the case design conveys high performance,
speed, and mobility. The interactive controls,
LCD status, and active display are located
in front and are slightly elevated for easy
actuation.

Product Thinking Mouse

Manufacturer Kensington Microware

Design firm Taylor & Chu

Designers Mark Edwards, Robin Chu, Neil Taylor, Chris Gadway

The Thinking Mouse fits comfortably in any hand, right or left, and has a rubberized overmolding for comfort and control. Another unique feature is the 2+2 programmable button arrangement. Two are for normal functions and the other two can be programmed for repetitive tasks, such as sending a fax, with a single click.

Product Network Executive *multimedia workstation*

Manufacturer New Network

Design firm I.D. Group International Inc.

Designers Daniel Koo, Jennyeu Weng

This customized workstation for mail uses a real-life graphic user-interface with sound and animation. Mail can be filed and accessed by a text-retrieval system. The color flat-panel display raises automatically, and the combined keyboard/trackball extends out when the unit is switched on.

Product	Integra-Media *multimedia personal computer*
Manufacturer	Fujitsu Ltd.
Design firm	Machineart
Designer	Andrew Serbinski

This product was designed for a creative person in graphics, advertising, or media production. To reduce the amount of desk space needed, the product is separated into two modules: the media module and the CPU/expansion unit. The small footprint media module and wireless keyboard/ mouse can be positioned off the work surface, while the CPU/expansion module can be placed in a remote location. The ability to separate the media drives from the processor is an innovation.

Product   Desktop Delivery *(concept)*
Manufacturer   AT&T Global Information Solutions
Design firm   AT&T Consulting Design Group
Designers   Jack Beduan, Donal Carr

Desktop Delivery revolutionizes an industry plagued
with look-alike hardware and endless software updates.
It redefines the notion of hardware and software as
separate entities, and delineates the PC's elements
according to the likelihood for the future change.
Borrowing from the imagery of software packaging,
the entire product is transformed in a visual expression
of its capabilities.

Product   PocketPro *interactive computer projector*
Manufacturer   Kopin Corporation
Design firm   Design Continuum
Designers   Michel Arney, Benjamin Beck, David Chastain, Greg Hunter

The PocketPro turns an ordinary slide projector into a computer-based
presentation system. The projection device allows for interactive,
computer-generated presentations. Weighing only a pound, the projector
is small enough to fit in a pocket and has no excess external features.

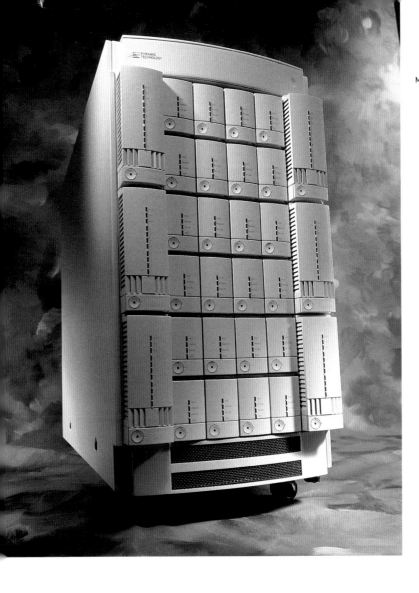

Product **Pyramid MESHine**
Manufacturer **Pyramid Technology**
Design firm **Palo Alto Design Group**
Designers **Malcom Smith, John Toor**

The Pyramid MESHine is a highly scalable computer system. Each cell can be stacked, and each drive module and CPU module is hot pluggable so that system shut down is not necessary.

Product **Gecko** *central processing unit*
Manufacturer **Hewlett Packard**
Design firm **ZIBA Design Inc.**
Designers **Sohrab Vossoughi, Mark Stella**

Gecko is a high-performance, low-cost CPU. Based on the user's preference, it can be positioned horizontally on the desk top or vertically on or under a work surface.

Product **Himalaya MPP** *parallel computer*
Manufacturer **Tandem Computers, Inc.**
Design firm **Tandem Industrial Design Group**
Designers **John Guenther, Ron Boeder**

This product uses the next generation technology to demonstrate the characteristics of Tandem's parallel-processing capability. The form makes a dramatic visual statement to underline the architectural and technological advantages of the product.

Product Digitizing Puck *cursor*

Manufacturer Houston Instruments

Design firm Design Edge

Designer Mark Kimbrough

This handheld digitizing cursor's asymmetrical design allows either hand to access all sixteen control buttons. A soft rubber welt encircles the grip for improved comfort and ease of use.

Product Color Stylewriter Pro *printer*

Manufacturer Apple Computer, Inc.

Design firm IDEO Product Development

Designers Christopher Loew, Tim Parsey (Apple Computer)

This is a quietly simple design. The only visible controls are the power-switch and paper-load lever, while various touchable forms suggest the functions, including the power button, cable connection, and front display tray.

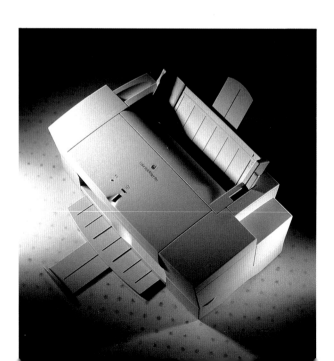

Product Eris *desktop video conferencing peripheral*

Manufacturer RSI

Design firm Worrell Design, Inc.

Designers Robert Worrel, James Luther

Eris is a Macintosh- and Windows-compatible peripheral product for desktop teleconferencing. Used in conjunction with a video camera, Eris makes a PC into a versatile and cost-effective teleconferencing tool. It uses both digital and standard phone lines, and is portable and easy to use.

FURNITURE

8

The focus on "soft" values in design inevitable comes to the subject of cultural expressiveness. Furniture design is one of the few areas of design remaining in which, as this section indicates, producers still engage the design services of those of their own nationality. The question is, can one discern a distinctly national design expression among this collection of recent designs. We leave it to the reader to decide.

Product **Suma Seating and Tables**

Manufacturer **Casas**

Design firm **Casas**

Designer **Óscar Tusquets Blanca**

Tandem seating assumes a fresh look, especially in the base splayed-foot supports. The configuration of the back supports, while designed for comfort, present a pleasant, undulating rhythm in the continuous, joined seats.

Product New Dimensions *furniture program*

Manufacturer Buck Meditintechnik, Berlin

Design firm Eckart & Barski Corporate Industrial Design

Designers Peter Ekert, Olaf Barski

While the design of this collection of nursing-care furniture does not connote "handicap," it is individually adjustable for a variety of handicaps and illnesses. Modular construction provides the requisite flexibility and ergonomic detailing in every furnishing component. A variety of colors and finishes injects a noninstitutional feel to the collection.

Product 341 Cos Chair

Manufacturer Cassina S.p.A.

Designer Josep Lluscà

Leather and wood are combined flawlessly in this series of conference chairs.

Product   Flo Armchair

Manufacturer   AXA

Design firm   Flores Associates

The sculptural shape and defined
separation between elements give
this chair a rich aesthetic character.

Product   Recycle Design Street Furniture

Manufacturer   Eaglebrook Products

Design firm   Fahnstrom McCoy

Designers   Dale Fahbstrom

This series of outdoor-amenities products is
focused on the goal of responsible design for
the environment. The client is in the business of
converting stream products into reprocessed
raw materials; its subsidiary produces a product
called Durawood, made from milk bottles. A
system of sand-cast aluminum structural components form the base for a variety of forms and
configurations for outdoor products such as
benches, planter boxes, and trash containers,
all of which make use of Durawood.

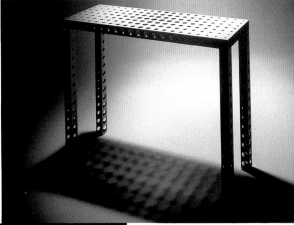

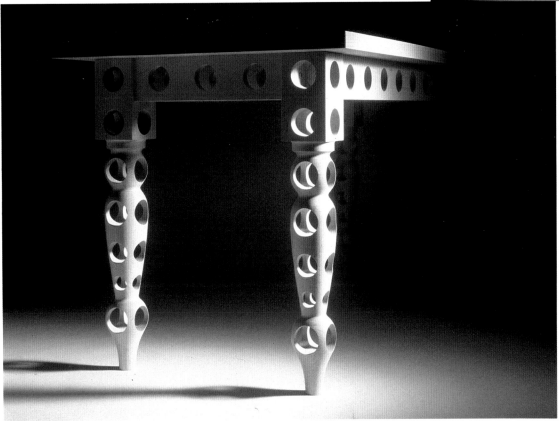

Product **Table-Console**

Manufacturer **Droog design**

Design firm **Gijs Bakker Design**

Designer **Gijs Bakker**

This table is part of a collection of furniture and interior accessories that explores the sense of material space invaded by the object. A series of progressively-sized holes is the visual theme for this expression.

Product **Dondolo Chair**

Manufacturer **Caimi Export S.p.A.**

Designer **Verner Panton**

The aluminum-tube-construction rocking chair with upholstered seat and back comes knocked down. ready for easy assembly.

Product **Faventia Chaise Longue**

Manufacturer Oken S.A.

Design firm Josep Lluscà Disseny Industrial SL

Designer Josep Lluscà

This lounge adjusts from a totally reclining to a more upright position.

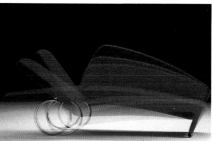

Product **Boulevard** *bistro-chair*

Manufacturer Ycami

Design firm Porsche Design GmbH

Designer Simon Fraser

In solving the client requirement of a weather and vandal-resistant aluminum chair for indoor-outdoor use, the simple two-part assembly of the seat and back was also a production efficiency bonus.

Product **Lizard Chair**

Manufacturer Fritz Hansen

Designer Torben Skov

This elegant, wooden chair is in the tradition of Danish craft.

Product Incisa Chair

Manufacturer De Padova

Designer Vico Magistretti

The upholstry detail endows this chair with elegance and a certain comfortable charm. The exterior, leather frame cover is stitched to create an organic, flowing pattern. The zippered covers are removable.

Product Louis 20 *chairs and table*

Manufacturer Vitra GmbH

Designer Philippe Starck

The one piece moulded-plastic seats of these chairs rest on the cast-aluminum rear legs. The profile presents an image of a human body sitting on the rear legs.

Product Leggero Armchair and Sofas

Manufacturer Cassina S.p.A.

Designer Massimo Iosa Ghini

This sofa is part of a seating series reminiscent of the early Eames and Saarinen designs of the 1940s: the designer was inspired by past but used contemporary materials.

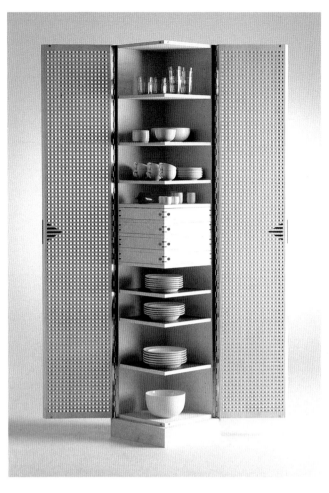

Product The Rabbit Chair

Designer Petri Vainio

This chair combines the rational and ergonomic solution with a humorous image of a rabbit. The unique support configuration for the back is achieved by the division in the middle, which allows the parts to be tilted toward one another.

Product Cupboard

Manufacturer Haslev Mobelsnedkeri

Design firm Design 134

The open-lattice door construction allows air circulation for this corner or freestanding cupboard.

Product Aero *table*

Manufacturer Casas

Design firm The Burdick Group

Designers Bruce and Susan Burdick

The aluminum cast support arms of the Aero base are all joined by an aluminum extrusion through a continuous slot that allows the table to be shipped in one flat package and assembled on site. The table top may be either wood or glass.

Product Opus Chair

Manufacturer Bent Krogh

Design firm Pelikan Design

The Opus is an injected plastic seat and back on a tubular metal frame.

Product Fractal Series *chair and table*

Manufacturer Flores Design Editions

Designer Kisho Kurokawa

Reminiscent of the Charles Eames molded plywood studies, this chair and table represent a contemporary Japanese view. The table is available in various sizes.

Product Lyon Theatre Seating

Manufacturer Figueras International Seating

Designer Jean Nouvel

This seating was designed for the Teatro de la Opera by its architect.

Product Lousiana Armchair

Manufacturer De Padova

Designer Vico Magistretti

The rigid leather outer shell and the fabric-removable inner cushions provide the comfort of traditional, large, cushy armchairs. The flowing, generous form of the chair, accentuated by the stitching of the leather shell, expresses its intended function—pure relaxation.

Product Nimbus Chair

Manufacturer Bent Krogh

Designers Gunvor & Niels Jorgen Haugesen

The Nimbus, an elegant plywood chair with a metal base and an optional seat pad demonstrates a mastery of wood design simplicity.

Product **Trinidad Chair**
Manufacturer **Fredericia Stolefabrik**
Designer **Nanna Ditzel**

This latest chair by Nanna Ditzel continues her long and successful history of Danish furniture design.

Product **Vilbert Chair**
Manufacturer **Ikea, Europe**
Designer **Verner Panton**

This is a knock-down chair made of MDF board, coated on both sides with high pressure laminates. It is available in two different 4-color combinations.

9

WORK TOOLS

"In the future, the whole scene of the office
will become very ambiguous, hybrid, uncertain.
Just as in the present metropolis, where we don't know anymore
if we are indoors or outdoors, at the bank, at the airport or at the hotel.
The future will offer very free and functional sites,
but with an 'identity low profile'."

Andrea Branzi

Product Citizen Office
Sponsor Vitra Museum
Designers Andrea Branzi, Michele De Lucchi, Ettore Sottsass

Ideas and Notes accompanying the environments designed
for the Citizen Office exhibition do not offer final solutions,
but present examples of a new approach to office culture.
The following are excerpts from the designers' notes:

The office is in a state of tremendous transition, not only because of the massive diffusion of
electronic equipment, but because of the changes in business organizations as they adapt to
the pressures of a global, post-industrial economy. Social and environmental issues are also
being brought to bear on traditional organizational structures, challenging the rigidity of time
and place of work. We are only at the threshold of these changes, and the opportunities for
designers to create new work environments and products are among the most exciting areas
of design for the new millennium.

There are many clues to new directions in office environment and product design in this
section. Andrea Branzi, Ettore Sottsass and Michele De Lucchi present their thinking in
"Citizen Office," an exhibition sponsored by the Vitra Museum in Weil am Rhein, Germany. In
viewing these prototypes, it is obvious that the ambience of the more comfortable informality
of the home is being applied to the office. Or are these prototypes, in fact, "home offices"?
The blurring of this distinction is one clue to the future.

Other products and environments in this section suggest the conflicting demands for private,
but very friendly, structured workspaces on the one hand, and flexible furnishings and accoutrements to accommodate continually re-forming work teams on the other hand.

Portability is a strong emerging design criterion, since workspaces are now varied as the
seat in an airport terminal, the chair in a hotel lobby, or the seat on a commuter train.

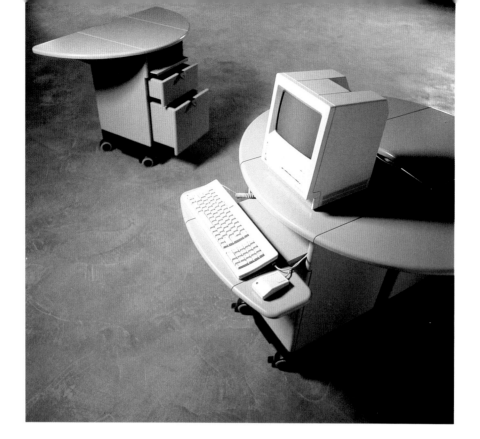

Product   Mobile Office Taboret System
Manufacturer   Egan Visual
Design firm   Kerr Keller Design
Designers   Miles Keller, Helen Kerr, Ingrid Reehill

These pieces are wired to support a range of electronic tasks and are available with different storage configurations. With their abbreviated wings unfurled, two semicircular units can be linked together to form a larger round work area. A rectangular piece can create a large meeting area, and when not in use, all pieces sit neatly folded on their sides.

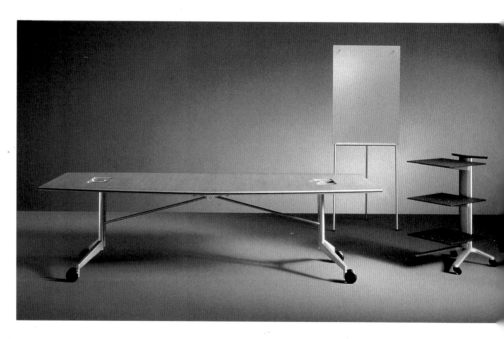

Product   Confair *conference products*
Manufacturer   Wilkhahn
Design firm   Wiege
Designers   Justus Kolberg, Jens Korte

Conferencing now encompasses a diversity of interactive modes of communicating and working. The Confair conferencing line anticipates a range of activities, furnishings, accessories, and arrangements that may be needed in a particular conference meeting.

Product **HÅG Scio rocking chair**

Manufacturer **HÅG**

Designer **Soren Yran**

The HÅG Scio is a very advanced rocking chair designed to smoothly follow the forward, backward, and sideways movement of the body. The seat and back are replaceable and all component parts are recyclable.

Product **Parachute Chair**

Manufacturer **The Knoll Group**

Design firm **DI Research and Design/Biomechanics Corporation of America**

Designer **Dragomir Ivicevic**

The Parachute was designed for small to mid-sized businesses that want a fully ergonomic, non-hierarchical chair. Research revealed that most office chair adjustment mechanisms are hard to understand and difficult to operate. Parachute's position adjustments were designed accordingly, with easy-to-use sculptural handles.

Product **Tutor Training Table System**

Manufacturer **Howe Furniture Corporation**

Design firm **Niels Diffrient Product Design**

Designers **Niels Diffrient, Robert Ferraro, Tom Latone**

This is a table-base system expressly designed for training activities. The centerpiece of the system is a single table in two widths. A number of accessory components permit an almost unlimited variety of training room set-ups.

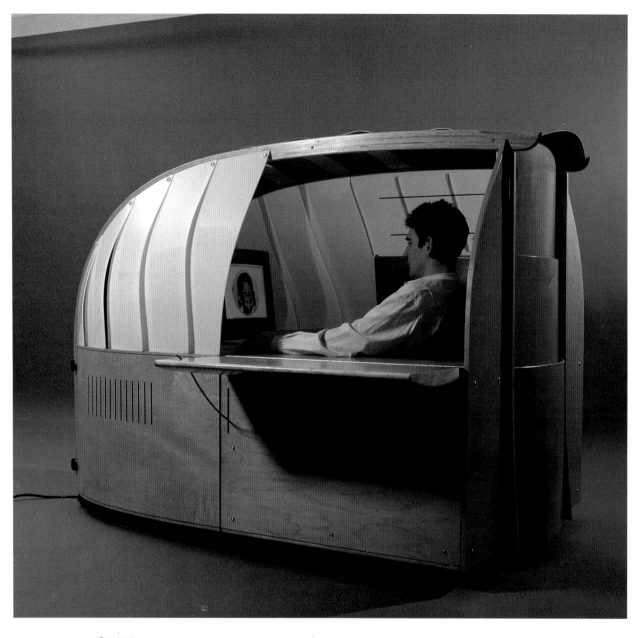

Product Clipper CS-I

Manufacturer Newspace, Inc., Division of Gilbert International

Design firm Douglas Ball, Inc.

Designers Douglas Ball, Leon Goldik, Jeff Sokalski

The computer worker enters his or her own capsule for a completely private, environmentally controlled workspace. This 1.2-meter-wide, 2.1-meter-long, and 1.4-meter-high capsule is entered like an automobile. It shuts out all distractions, offers diffused lighting, and has an integrated, yet flexible ergonomic seat and computer worksurface.

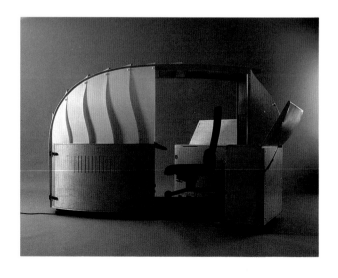

Product **Knoll Tables**

Manufacturer **Knoll Group**

Design firm **Knoll**

Designer **Carl Magnusson**

These conference tables feature unique cable management capabilities: grooves within the mast legs accommodate data and communications wiring.

Product **Personal Harbor® Workspace**

Manufacturer **Steelcase Inc.**

Design firm **Steelcase Research & Development/Industrial Design**

Designers **William Miller (R&D), Dave Lathrop (Program Management)**

Mark Baloga, Paul Siebert, Steven Eriksson (Industrial Design)

Photographer **Hedrich-Blessing**

This concept was shaped by the image of tents around a campfire. Boundaries between private and group activities can be controlled by the individual with such traditional architectural devices as a front porch (a 30.5-cm to 121.9-cm extended space in front of each Personal Harbor) and a door.

Product TD Collection™ *home office furniture*

Manufacturer Herman Miller, Inc.

Designers Tom Newhouse, Don Shepherd

Made of solid cherry hardwood, this collection includes a compact work desk with folding leaves and a hinged, two-position display easel. Filing/storage cabinets, book and computer shelves, and accessories can be added as needed. The product is lightweight and partially disassembles for ease of transport in residential environments. The collection's slim, friendly look enhances its compatibility with residential furniture.

Product T-chair

Manufacturer Vitra GmbH

Design firm Antonio Citterio

Designers Antonio Citterio, Glen Oliver Low

The blurred border between living and working environments is evident in this chair, which, with its fresh appearance, would be at home in either place. A new upholstery technique allows the chair cover to be taken off like a T-shirt and laundered in the washing machine. The armrest platform, which can be adjusted in its height, width, or angle, provides welcome arm-leaning support.

Product **Modus** *office chair*

Manufacturer **Wilkhahn**

Design firm **Wiege**

Designers **Fritz Frenkler, J. Kolberg, K. Frank, W. Sauer**

Wilkhahn's development of its "dynamic sitting" concept, in which a syn-chro-mechanism allows one to shift positions without adjusting levers and screws, continues with the introduction of the Modus as an evolutionary design in the succession of chairs. This design pays attention to environ-mental issues by streamlining components and materials as well as struc-turing with demountable joints.

Product **Ad Hoc-Office System**

Manufacturer **VITRA GmbH**

Design firm **Antonio Citterio**

Designers **Antonio Citterio, Glenn Oliver Low**

This lighthearted office system could have been inspired by the Eames Storage Units (ESU) of the late 1940s, with its perforated sur-faces, bright colors, and general openness. This is a product that can work in the " Bureaulandschaft," open landscape environment.

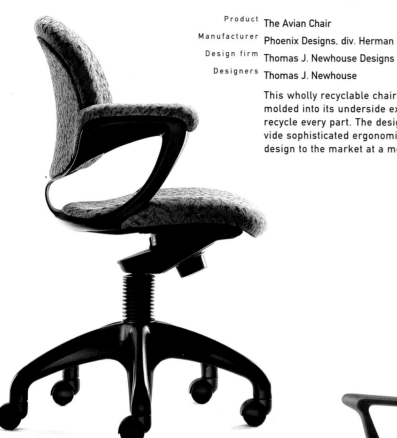

Product The Avian Chair
Manufacturer Phoenix Designs, div. Herman Miller Inc.
Design firm Thomas J. Newhouse Designs
Designers Thomas J. Newhouse

This wholly recyclable chair includes a chart molded into its underside explaining how to recycle every part. The design focus is to provide sophisticated ergonomic and visual design to the market at a moderate priced.

Product Vertair Office Seating
Manufacturer Castelli, Italy
Design firm Emilio Ambasz & Associates Inc.
Designer Emilio Ambasz

This chair's patented upholstery system, made of narrow, overlapping bands of leather stitched to elastic bands, formally expresses the chair's flexibility to changing body movement. The chair combines a soft-tech look with high-tech performance.

Product HÅG Signet *office chair*
Manufacturer HÅG
Design firm Svein Asbornsen & Partners

This high-back executive chair is designed for people who spend a large part of the working day leaning back. The adjustable neck and lumbar support are unique to the HÅG product line.

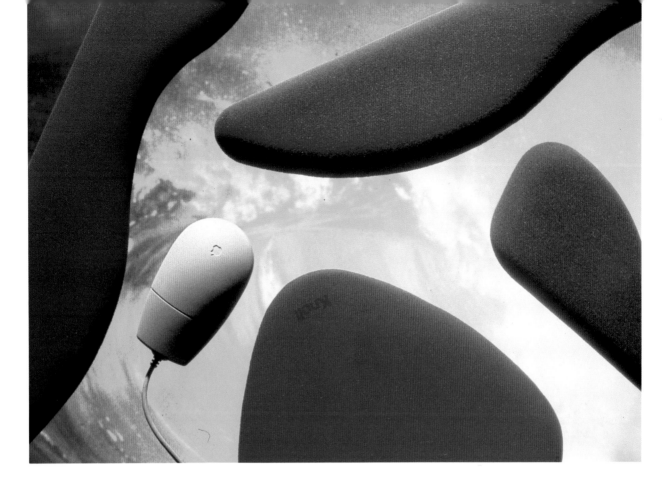

Product Surf Collection
Manufacturer The Knoll Group
Design firm VENT/X
Designers Ross Lovegrove, Stephen Peart

This amorphic collection, which consists of wrist rest, mouse pad, foot rest, lumbar support, and a "surf board" corner unit, has raised desktop design standards. Dense, GECET™ material provides excellent energy absorption as the user applies pressure. An outer layer of Neoprene offers resilient cushioning for hands and feet. The surf board corner unit, with its rolled front and rubberized bumpers, provides a larger space extension than is usual.

Product Alfax *desktop accessories*
Manufacturer Hoyo
Design firm Ecco Design Inc.
Designer Jeff Miller

A wave motif visually integrates performance and aesthetics into a single theme for paper trays and other supply holders. These accessories are spacesaving and can be stacked and snapped in a variety of configurations.

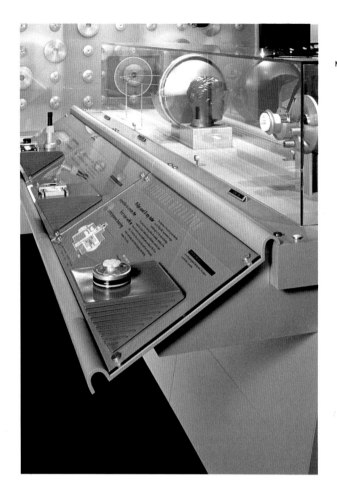

Product   Philips Center of Competence Special
Purpose Furniture

Manufacturer   Carlton Benbow Contracts, England;
Gielissen BV, The Netherlands

Design firm   The Burdick Group

Designers   Bruce Burdick, Susan K. Burdick, Bruce Lightbody,
Jon Betthauser and Team, Robert Blaich (Design
Director, Philips)

This system design was originally created
for an exhibition facility. Armatures are fabri-
cated in aluminum and steel. A central
channel-and-bracket system provides support
for top surfaces, and vertical panels define
graphic displays.

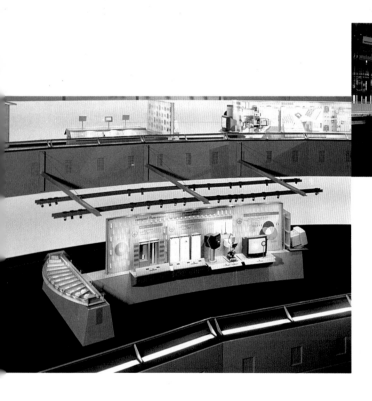

Product Aeron™ *chair*

Manufacturer Herman Miller, Inc.

Designers Don Chadwick, Bill Stumpf

The Aeron™ chair uses a completely new system of body support with its resilient Pellicle™ membrane, which distributes weight evenly over the seat pan and backrest. Unlike foam and fabric, this membrane "breathes", preventing hot-weather discomfort. The new Kinematic™ tilt mechanism allows the user to assume a range of positions, while the chair design accommodates a wide variety of body types.

GOOD
GOODS

10

Product Drawing Tubes
Design firm NCS Design Rio
Designers Celso M. Santos, Alexander Neumeister

My friend and mentor, Charles Eames, often used the term "Good Goods." His close associates knew exactly what he meant—a kind of shorthand for objects that one just looks at and, without a lot of analysis, knows it's good. The Good Goods, in Charles's mind, uncompromisingly met the highest standards of design; these were objects he would like to own and surround himself with. I have always liked the term Good Goods. After studying the large number of entries for this book, it seemed to me that there were some small, everyday objects that were quite simply Good Goods. These are things I would enjoy having or using. I hope Charles would agree.

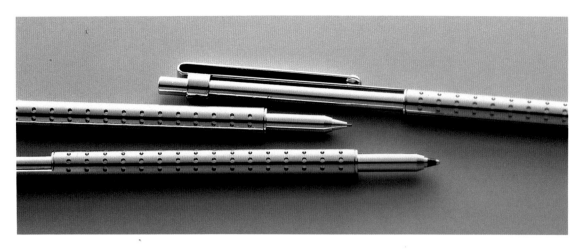

Product Lamy Spirit *ballpoint pen,*
mechanical pencil
Manufacturer Lamy
Design Group Lamy
Designer Wolfgang Fabian

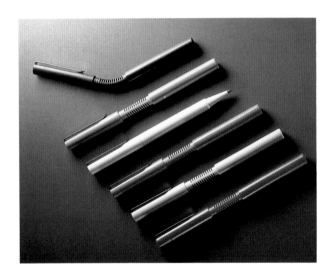

Product Flexiboll Ballpoint Pen
Manufacturer Pentel
Design firm Emilio Ambasz & Associates, Inc.
Designer Emilio Ambasz

Product Meganetta *reading glasses*
Manufacturer Avanti Inc.
Design firm Igarashi Studio
Designer Takenobu Igarashi

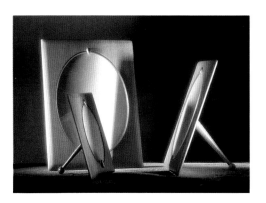

Product Alante *picture frame*
Manufacturer Rede Guzzini SRL
Designer Luciano Altesini

Product Shachihata Wevox Stationery Line
Designer frogdesign inc.

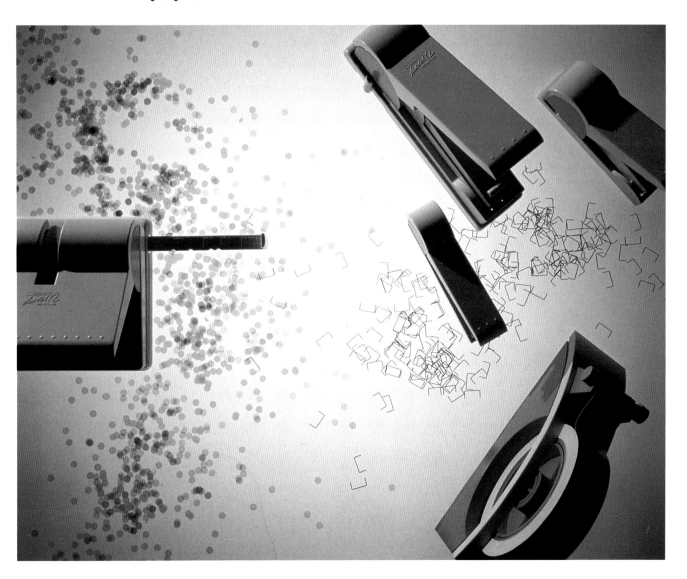

Product Mixing Jug
Manufacturer Royal Copenhagen
Designer Jørgen Møller

Product Stainless Dinnerware
Manufacturer Tsubame Shinko Industrial Co., Ltd.
Design firm Igarashi Studio
Designer Takenobu Igarashi

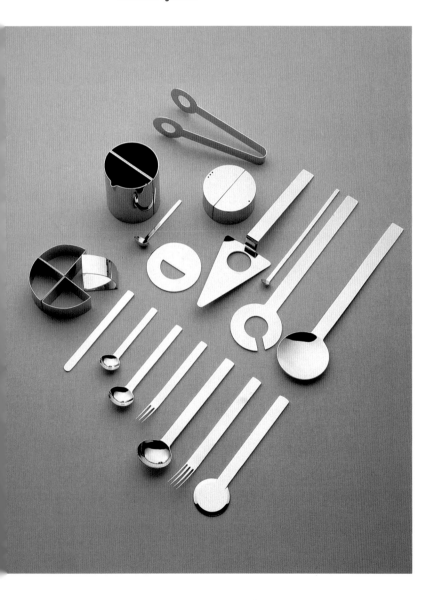

Product Generation and Communication *glassware lines*
Manufacturer Jenaer Glaswerke
Design firm frogdesign inc.

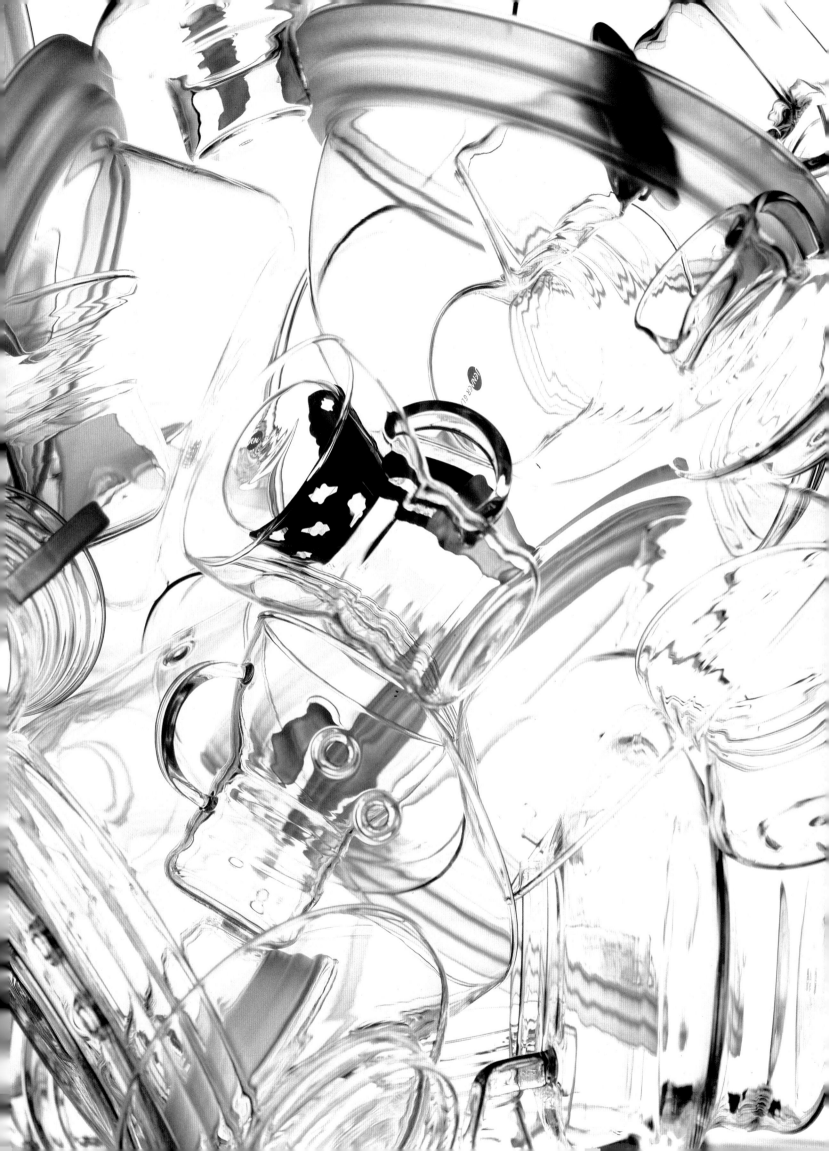

Product Vercingetorige *alarm clock*
Manufacturer Rexite S.p.A. Milan, Italy
Design firm Studio Brown
Designer Julian Brown

Product O'Clock *alarm clock*
Manufacturer Rede Guzzini SRL
Design firm Luciano Altesini Design
Designer Luciano Altesini

Product Analogous Watch
Manufacturer Lou Beeren
Design firm Lou Beeren Industrial Design
Designers Lou Beeren, Peter Stut

Product Wrist Watch
Manufacturer Crival Ltd., Switzerland
Design firm Verner Panton
Designer Verner Panton

Product Braun Time Control
Manufacturer Braun A.G.
Design Group Braun Design Department
Designer Dietrich Lubs

Product ECX 1 Panorama *camera*
Manufacturer Samsung Aerospace Ind. Ltd.
Design firm Porsche Design GmbH
Designer Christian Schwamkrug

Product Fotoman
Manufacturer Logitech
Design firm Montgomery Pfeiffer

Product Compakt CD Holder
Manufacturer Dibis Inc.
Design firm Dibis Inc.
Designer Michael Santella

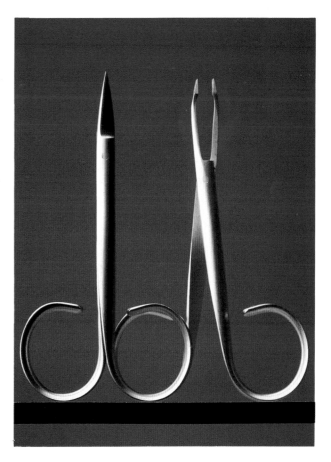

Product RSC *nail scissors, tweezers*
Manufacturer Rubis S.A.
Design firm Stabio/Switzerland

STUDENT
WORK

The designers who will be taking us into the millennium are today's students. Students' relative freedom to explore dramatically new directions provides a rich source for challenging the status quo, not only in visual expression, but in the kinds of products they choose to create. Many of the projects in this section are totally new kinds of products. Marketing managers and product planners, take note.

Student freedom to explore, however, is not entirely without constraints. More and more projects are linked to corporate sponsorship. Students do understand that there are practical development, production, and marketing objectives within which businesses must operate.

The international group of design schools in this section demonstrates that student designers do not necessarily reflect a "national" design language characteristic. In fact, within design schools themselves, the students are culturally diverse. There may even be a "school culture" as a result of the direction of professors' leadership and interaction among student peer groups.

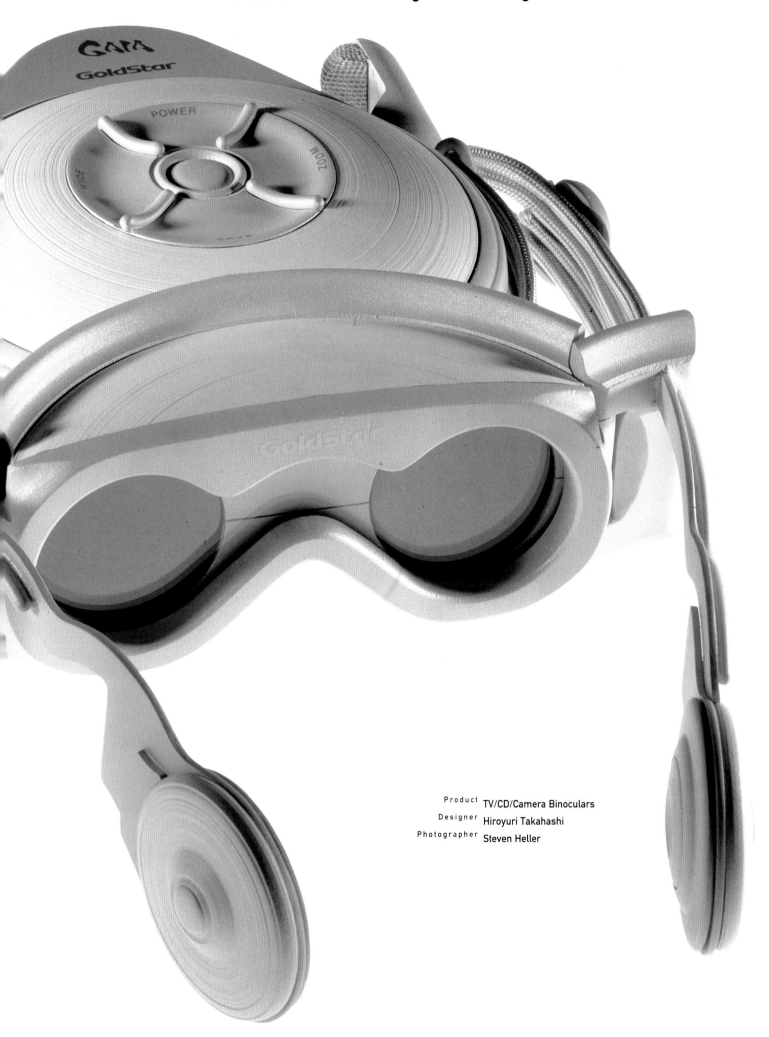

Product TV/CD/Camera Binoculars
Designer Hiroyuri Takahashi
Photographer Steven Heller

Product Pindar *digital camera*

Designer Erik Kiaer

This camera is designed to share images with people the photographer meets along the way.

Institute of Design/ITT

Product Electronic Magazine

Designer Douglas Cook

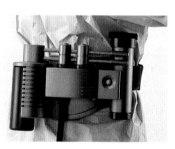

Product Organic Vapor Analyzer

Designer Paul R. Herrold Jr.

The difficult conditions of hazardous vapor measurement are alleviated by OVA, which holds the user instead of the user holding the equipment.

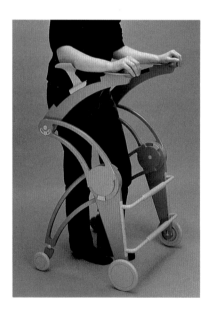

Product Footpath *walking aid*

Designer John C. Whiteman

An assisting device designed in the form of human skeletal structure, this walking aid is a metaphoric extension of the body. Ergonomic forms adjust to user's posture and balance needs, the almost playful appearance encourages use-acceptance.

Product Eastman *tourist device*

Designer Sven Adolph

This combination elec-
tronic camera and "global
positioning" tourist guide
is clad in leather to wear
well over time.

Cranbrook Academy of Art

Product The Media Blanket *audio/video unit*

Designer Mark Stockwell

For this audio/video blanket that users
can wrap up in, the electronics are
woven into the felt.

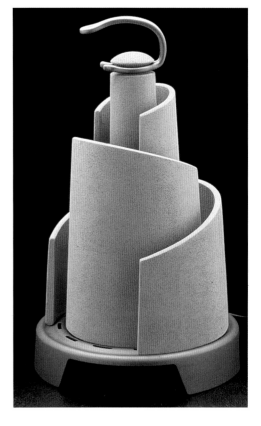

Product Electric Heater

Designer Sven Adolph

Product Electronic Wallet

Designer Tom Bouchard

This electronic credit and debit
card graphs user's account
balance and money spent.

Cranbrook Academy of Art

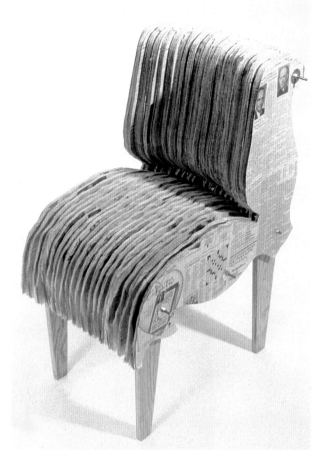

Product The Paper Chair
Designer Michael Culpepper

Newspapers cut to shape and bolted together create a chair that you can read and recycle.

Product Sopus *alarm/reading light pillow*
Designer Howard M. Montgomery

Theories concerning human need for light inspired this concept for an ambient, switch-on sun.

Product Jack *multipurpose tool*
Designer Sven Adolph

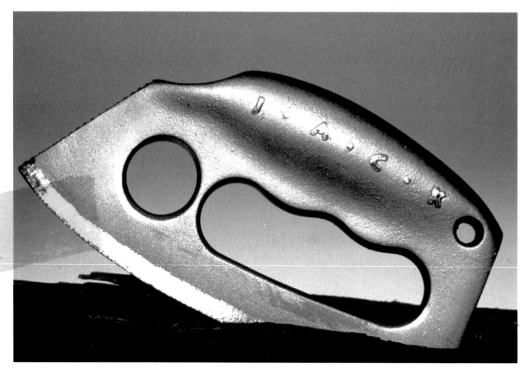

Product The Information Tapestry *liquid crystal display*

Designer Abigail Shachat

Fifteen-centimeter square, color LCD screens
are woven into large sheets that can be hung
between floor and ceiling, creating an electronic architecture.

Product Domestic Computer Display

Designers Michael Culpepper, Richard Bates

A vinyl beanbag houses this computer for the elderly. The soft casing adds a domestic element to a
traditionally industrial product.

Product End Table

Designer Robert Rabinovitz

A kinetic object that oscillates, this table is a
study in appreciation of flexible materials.

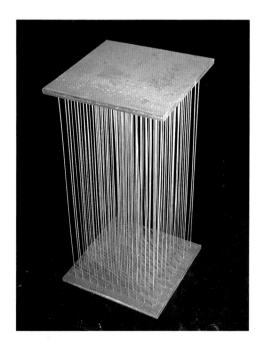

Product Playing in the System *meditation table and chairs*

Designer Robert Rabinovitz

Intended to explore the human condition of
sensorial phenomena.

University of the Arts

Product   Interchangeable Scissors
Designer John Choi

Scissor blades can be turned for use in the opposite direction.

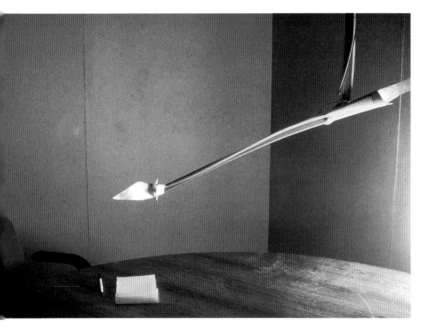

Product   Snap Modular Lighting System
Designer Todd Corlett

The lightweight task- and spot lights of this system can illuminate an entire room.

Product   Collapsible Ice Axe
Designer Jason Clarke

This mountain-climbing tool collapses, fitting easily into any outdoor pack.

Product Personal Interactive Television Broadcaster

Designer Michael Schmick

This broadcaster attaches to any television set to interrupt, interact, and program.

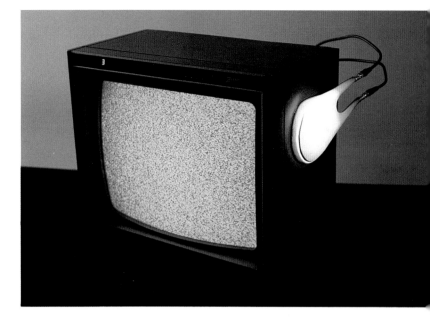

Product Bicycle Brake System

Designer Jason Clark

The tensile strength of the lightweight aluminum provides a stronger bicycle brake with less weight than standard brakes.

Product Orly *high-touch lamp*

Designers Tony Leo, Tony Wurman

The Orly lamp is adjustable for ambient or task use.

Product Multipurpose Knife

Designer Tony Leo

This utility two-sided knife/saw has four cutting edges. Its handle flips to provide different blades and splits to cover blades.

California State University/Long Beach

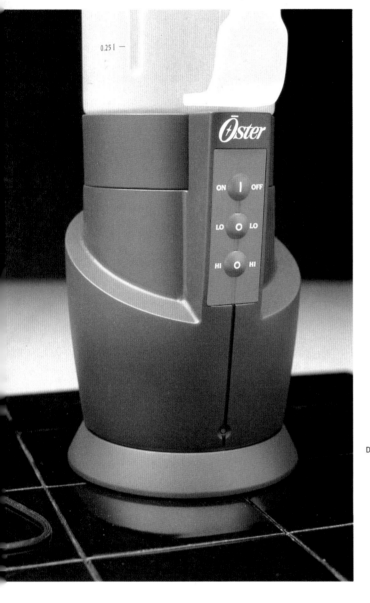

Product Osiris Field Information Exchange

Designer Joseph A. Cesario

The ability to write directly on the computer screen encourages archaeologists to use available technology for gathering geographic data.

Product Oster Dual Speed Blender

Designers Michael Kammermeyer, Joseph A. Cesario

This redesign of a ubiquitous product includes a container that locks onto the motor for hands-free use. Attention was paid to spill cleaning problems, while the aesthetics were updated to encourage on-counter storage.

Product Ant Eater *picnic table*

Designers Larry McKinney, Trung Q. Phung

This playful and functional design reinterprets of the standard bench-style picnic table.

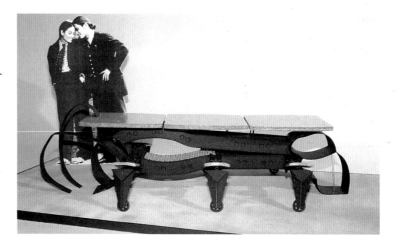

Product Peg-E *modular bookcase*

Designer Trung Q. Phung

The small-space shelving system is portable and includes flexible shelving made of recycled fiberboard.

Product Stratabox Media Storage Racks

Designer Jeff Meridith

Die-cut corrugated cardboard forms a compact disc and VHS tape rack.

Product Survival Kit

Designers David Yim, Trung Q. Phung

Re-examining assistance tools for outdoor activities, this kit anticipates emergency situations with user-efficient design details. The flashlight body can be operated and used without removing it from the kit shell. The entire kit hooks easily onto most ropes, clips, and packs for easy carrying.

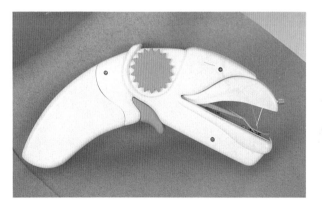

Product Handheld Sewing Machine

Designer Laura Caghan

The design of existing sewing machines was improved by simplifying threading and reducing wrist and arm strain.

Art Center College of Design/Pasadena

Product **Task Light**
Designer **Jovo Majstorovic**
Photographer **Steven Heller**

The task light's wearable light pack houses both the battery and pin-point directed light.

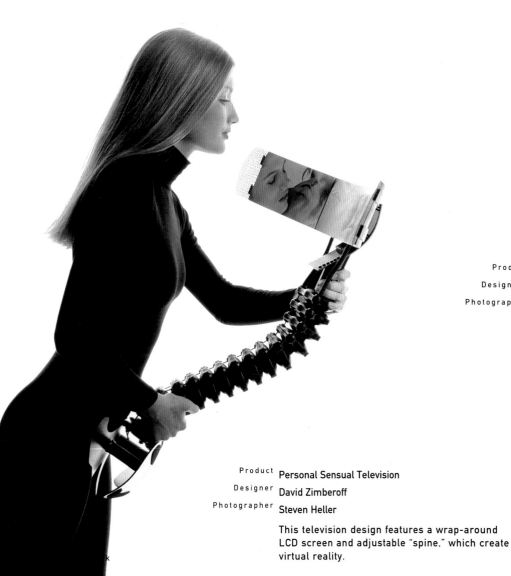

Product **6-D Computer Input Device/Game Controller**
Designers **Joe Tan, John Guerra**
Photographer **Steven Heller**

The game controller's emphasis is on intuitive operation and human factors.

Product **Personal Sensual Television**
Designer **David Zimberoff**
Photographer **Steven Heller**

This television design features a wrap-around LCD screen and adjustable "spine," which create virtual reality.

Product Photojournalist Camera
Designer Rpin Suwannath
Photographer Steven Heller

Expansive shapes and textures create an easy-to-use, portable tool.

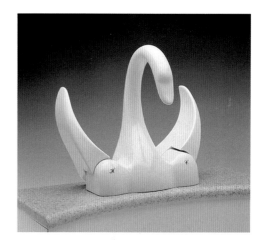

Product Swan Faucet
Designer James Wilson
Photographer Steven Heller

This elegant, neo-Victorian design metaphor executes art from a simple bathroom fixture.

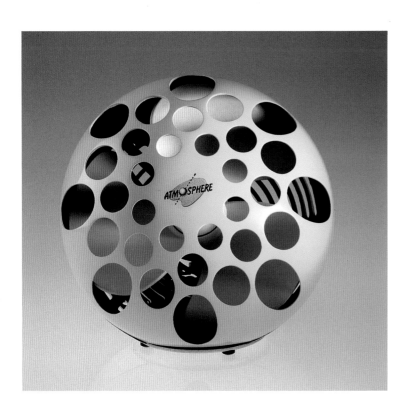

Product Atmosphere *personal fan*
Designer Gerry Meyer
Photographer Steven Heller

Playful shapes and colors update the traditional fan, while circular vents replace the standard, symmetrical lines.

Art Center of Design/Europe

Product Russian Radio
Designer Hannes Weibel

Product Police Walkie-Talkie
Designer Pietro Bottone

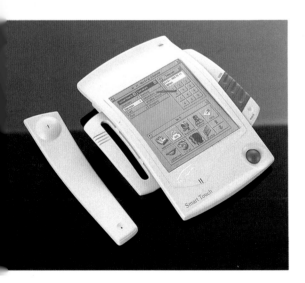

Product Photo Touch Telephone for Elderly People
Designer Satyendra Pakhale
Photographer Fabrice Bettex

Familiar forms and simplicity of use organize the number of electronic resources this smart phone offers.

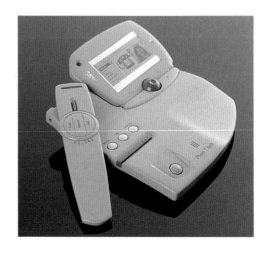

Product Smart Touch *digital telephone for home*
Designer Satyendra Pakhale
Photographer Fabrice Bettex

Product Act Two *interactive audio/video entertainment system*
Designer Vladimir Zinovieff

Act Two encourages a mixture of acting and Karaoke, in which the user becomes an actor.

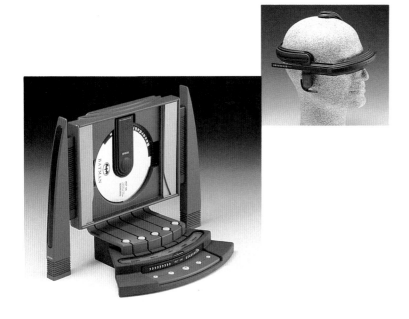

Product Stackable Chair
Designer Hannes Weibel

Product Gynecological Examination Chair
Designer Stephanie Henze

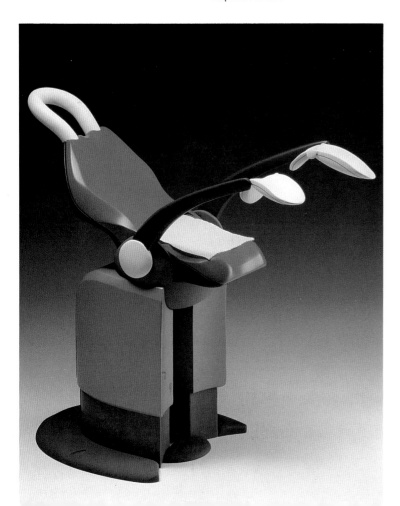

Product Insight *digital radio*
Designer Satyendra Pakhale
Photographer Fabrice Bettex

This radio design explores the potential of digital technology for future needs.

Product Video Tent *two-way video communicator*
Designer Anthony Di Bitonto

This two-way video communicator makes the images of all participants visible. The communicants' faces are superimposed against the present background image.

Pratt Institute

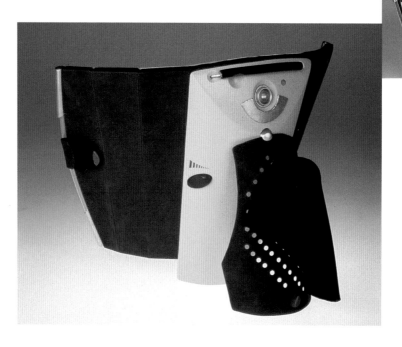

Product The Voyager Collection™ *electronic accessories*
Designer Erin Hoover

Voyager's wearable electronic accessories (Wrist guide, Camera Cap, Satellite Shoes, Datascarf) are designed for the challenges of travel.

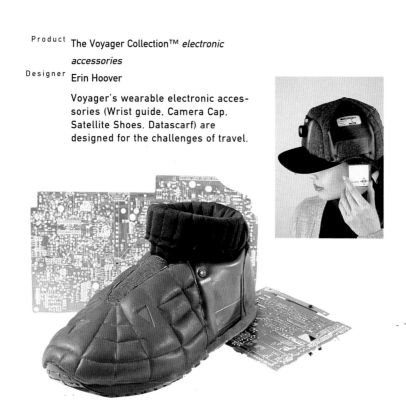

Product Dijit *electronic wallet*
Designer Leslie Muller

This electronic wallet is used with a smart card and thumbprint for scanner recognition.

Product Solar Tree *solar power system*
Designers James Bender, Chris Roat,
Dargen Moore

This main power system for electric
car stations is part of a Ford electric
car program.

North Carolina State

Product Organo *folding wooden chair*
Designer Stephan Schönherr

This unique design redefines the traditional
folding chair with the use of only three feet,
a circular back, and wheels.

Product Auto Card *parking meter*
Designer Henry Brink

This solar-powered parking meter
operates with a magnetic card.

Product Aura *mood enhancer*
Designer Bryant Cole

The Aura is a multi-modal therapeutic
device for executive stress management.

Western Washington University

Product **Electric Pencil Sharpener**
Designer Kevin Byrd Murray

A new take on the usual black box.

Product Twist 'N Sip *water purifier*
Designer Daniel Friedlander

This purifier uses iodide-saturated cloth for purification. while a carbon filter eliminates taste and odor.

Product Cantilevered Paintbrush
Designer Kevin Byrd Murray

For artists who prefer to paint from the back of the brush, the fulcrum of this brush is placed aft for improved balance.

University of Industrial Arts Helsinki

Product **Electronic Book**
Designers **Tommi Johannsson, Iikka Husgafvel**

Product **Grain** *attachable lamp*
Designers **Ilona Törmikoski, Paula Junttila**

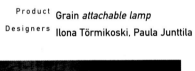

Product **Salt Dispenser**
Designer **Lin Ming-Huang**

The form of this dispenser is based on Chinese cultural metaphors.

Product **Multi-Purpose Ski Boot**
Designer **Juha Kosonen**

The boot can be used for downhill, cross-country, and telemark skiing.

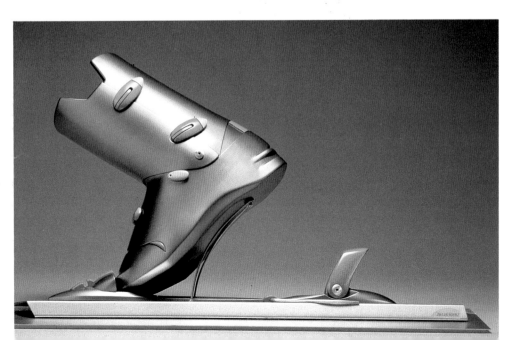

INDEX & DIRECTORY

Sven Adolph
Cranbrook Academy of Art
1221 N. Woodward
Bloomfield Hills, MI 48304

Alessi Design
Alessi SpA
Via Prirata Alessi 6
28023 Crusinallo Di Omega
Italy

Luciano Altesini
Via Le Grazie, 31
62019 Recanati
Italy

Ampex Corporate Industrial Design
401 Broadway
Redwood City, CA 94063

Apple Computer Inc.
20730 Valley Green Drive
Cupertino, CA 95014

Josep Aregall
Metalarta, S.A.
Avda. Barcelona 4
08970 Sant Joan Despi
Barcelona
Spain

Ashcraft Design
11832 W. Pico Boulevard
Los Angeles, CA 90064

AT&T Consulting Design Group
1700 S. Patterson Boulevard
Dayton, OH 45479

J. Auge
Leopoldo Mila DAE
Poligono Industrial Sant Jordi S N
08800 Vilanova I La Geltru
Barcelona
Spain

The Axis Group Inc.
65 Bellwoods Avenue
Toronto, Ontario M6J 3N4
Canada

Richard Bates
Cranbrook Academy of Art
1221 N. Woodward
Bloomfield Hills, MI 48304

James Bender
School of Design/NCSU
Raleigh, NC 27695

Bissell Industrial Design Group
P.O. Box 1888
Grand Rapids, MI 49501

BOLT (formerly Machen Montague)
2221 Edge Lake Drive, Suite 100
Charlotte, NC 28217

Pietro Bottone
Art Center College of Design (Europe)
Château de Sully,
Route de Chaily 144
Case Postale 32,
1814 La Tour-de-Peilz
Switzerland

Tom Bouchard
Cranbrook Academy of Art
1221 N. Woodward
Bloomfield Hills, MI 48304

Andrea Branzi
Vitra GmbH
Charles Eames-Strasse 2
D-79576 Weil am Rhein
Germany

Braun Design Department
Braun A.G.
Frankfurter Strasse 145
D-61476 Kronberg
Germany

Henry Brink
School of Design/NCSU
Raleigh, NC 27695

Peter Bysted
Danish Design Center
HC Andersens Boulevard 18
DK 1553 Copenhagen V
Denmark

Laura Caghan
Industrial Design Department
California State Long Beach
3859 E. 8th Street
Long Beach, CA 90804

Casas
Pol. Santa Rita
0875 Castellbisbal
Barcelona
Spain

Joseph A. Cesario
Industrial Design Department
California State Long Beach
3859 E. 8th Street
Long Beach, CA 90804

Cesaroni Design Associates Inc.
1865 Grove Street
Glenview, IL ZIP 60025

Donald Chadwick Associates
2050 Broadway
Santa Monica, CA 90404

Dennis Chan
Cetra
Sung Shan Terminal
340 Tun Hwan Road
Taipei 10592, R.O.C.

John Choi
University of the Arts
Industrial Design Department
310 S. Broad Street
Philadelphia, PA 19102

Ciro Design
192 Technology Drive
Unit E
Irvine, CA 92718

Antonio Citterio
Vitra GmbH
Charles Eames-Strasse 2
D-79576 Weil am Rhein
Germany

Jason Clark
The University of the Arts
Industrial Design Department
320 South Broad Street
Philadelphia, PA 19102

Franco Clivio
Erco Leuchter G.m.b.H.
Postfach 2460
5850 Lüdensheid
Germany

Bryant Cole
School of Design/NCSU
Raleigh, NC 27695

Douglas Cook
Institute of Design
Illinois Institute of Technology
10 W. 35th Street
Chicago, IL 60614

Todd Corlott
The University of the Arts
Industrial Design Department
320 South Broad Street
Philadelphia, PA 19102

Michael Culpepper
Cranbrook Academy of Art
1221 N. Woodward
Bloomfield Hills, MI 48304

Datascope Corporate Design
14 Philips Parkway
Montvale, NJ 07645

Michele DeLucchi
Vitra GmbH
Charles Eames-Strasse 2
D-79576 Weil am Rhein
Germany

Design Central
68 W. Whittier Street
Columbus, OH 43206

Design Continuum Inc.
648 Beacon Street
Boston, MA 02215

Design Edge, Austin TX
1205 Rio Grande Street
Austin, TX 78701

Anthony Di Bitonto
136 Hicks Street #2B
Brooklyn, NY 11201

Dibis Inc.
C.P. 1323 Place Bonaventure
Montreal, Quebec, Canada

Dictaphone Industrial Design Group
3191 Broadbridge Avenue
Stratford, CT 06497

DI Research and Design/
Biomechanics Corporation
of America, Knoll Group
105 Wooster Street
New York, NY 10012-3808

Nanna Ditzel
Danish Design Center
HC Andersens Boulevard 18
DK 1553 Copenhagen V
Denmark

dok Produkt Ontwerpers
Entrepotdok 20
1018 AD Amsterdam
The Netherlands

Douglas Ball Inc.
178 Senneville Road
Senneville
Quebec H9X 3L2, Canada

E & D Design OY
Juhana Hertuan Puistokalu 19
20100 Turku, Finland

Ecco Design Inc.
89 Fifth Ave., Suite 600
New York, NY 10003

Eckart & Barski Corporate
Industrial Design
Deutschherrnufer 32-D
60594 Frankfurt, Germany

Emilio Ambasz & Associates Inc.
636 Broadway
New York, NY 10012

ERCO Design
Erco Leuchter G.m.b.H.
Postfach 2460
5850 Lüdensheid, Germany

Fahnstrom/McCoy
954 W. Washington
Chicago, IL 60607

A. Ferrer
Leopoldo Mila DAE
Poligono Industrial Sant Jordi S N
08800 Vilanova I La Geltru
Barcelona, Spain

Fiskars Design
Fin-10330
Billnäs, Finland

Fitch Inc.
10350 Olentangy River Road
Worthington, OH 43085

Flores Associats
Argenters, Edif. 2
Parc Tecnològic
Barcelona, Spain

Frechin et Bureau
92 Rue de Crinee
75019 Paris
France

Daniel Friedlander
Western Washington University
304 36th Street #243
Bellingham, WA 98225

frogdesign inc.
1325 Chesapeake Terrace
Sunnyvale, CA 94089

Garcia Garay SL
San Antonlo 13
Sta Coloma Grment
Spain

Massimo Iosa Ghini
c/o Cassini S.p.A.
Via Busnell 1, Italy

Gijs Bakker Design
1017 Ek
Amsterdam

Ginko Design Inc.
130 Perry Street
San Francisco, CA 94107

Goldsmith Yamasaki Specht Inc.
900 N. Franklin Street
Chicago, IL 60610

Jon Guerra
Art Center College of Design
1700 Lida Street
Pasadena, CA 91103

Hari & Associates Inc.
3915 Howard Street
Skokie, IL 60076

Stephanie Henze
Art Center College of Design (Europe)
Château de Sully
Route de Chaily 144
Case Postale 32
1814 La Tour-de-Peilz
Switzerland

Paul R. Herold Jr.
Institute of Design
Illinois Institute of Technology
10 W. 35th Street
Chicago, IL 60614

Hiroyuri Takahashi
Art Center College of Design
1700 Lida Street
Pasadena, CA 91103

Hollington Associates
66 Leonard Street
London EC2A 4QX, England

Erin Hoover
Pratt Institute
396 Broome Street #16
New York, NY 10013

Isao Hosoe, Architect
c/o Luxo Italiana S.p.A.
Via Delle More #1
Presezzo, Bergamo, Italy

Iikka Husgafvel
University of Art & Design Helsinki
Hameentie 135 C
00560 Helsinki, Finland

ID Group International Inc.
Tun Hwa South Road 205
Section 1, 16th Floor
Taipei, Taiwan

IBM Corporation
In-House Design
3605 Highway 52 N.
Rochester, MN 55901

IDEO Product Development
78 Jeffreys Place
Jeffreys Street
London, NW1 9PP
England

Igarashi Studio
6-6-22 Minami-Aoyama
Minato-ku, Tokyo 107, Japan

Ingo Maurer GmbH
Kaisterstrasse 47
80801 Munich, Germany

Interform
3475 Edison Way, Building F
Menlo Park, CA 94025

Tommi Johannsson
University of Art & Design Helsinki
Hameentie 135 C
00560 Helsinki, Finland

Josep Llusca Disseny Industrial SL
Mamella 4
08023 Barcelona, Spain

Juha Kosonen
University of Art & Design Helsinki
Hameentie 135 C
00560 Helsinki, Finland

Paula Junttila
University of Art & Design Helsinki
Hameentie 135 C
00560 Helsinki, Finland

Michael Kammermeyer
Industrial Design Department
California State Long Beach
3859 E. 8th Street
Long Beach, CA 90804

Kan Industrial Designers
145 W. 27th Street W.
New York, NY 10001

Karim Rashid Industrial Design
145 27th Street #45
New York, NY 10001

Kerr Keller Design
1977 Queen Street E.
Toronto, Ontario, Canada

Erik Kiaer
Institute of Design
Illinois Institute of Technology
10 W. 35th Street.
Chicago, IL 60614

The Knoll Group
105 Wooster Street
New York, NY 10012

Linda A. Kuo
123 W. 13th Street, #602
New York, NY 10011

Kisho Kurokawa
Flores Design Edition
Benratherstrasse #6
D-40213 Dusseldorf
Germany

Lamy
G. Josef Lamy, GmbH
D-69111 Heidelberg
Germany

Tony Leo
The University of the Arts
Industrial Design Department
320 South Broad Street
Philadelphia, PA 19102

David Lewis
Bang & Olufsen
Peter Bangs Veu 15
DK-7600 Struer
Denmark

Lin Ming-Huang
University of Art & Design Helsinki
Hameentie 135 C
00560 Helsinki, Finland

Philip T.K. Lin
Cetra
Sung Shan Terminal
340 Tun Hwan Road
Taipei 10592 R.O.C.

Josep Llusca
Disseny Industrial S.L.
Mamella 408023 Barcelona
Spain

Lou Beeren Industrial Design
Verlengde Hereweg T31
9721 Al. Groningen
The Netherlands

Francesco Lucchese Architect
Luxo Italiana S.p.A.
Via Delle More 1
Presezzo, Bergamo, Italy

Luciano Altesini Design
Via Le Grazie, 31
62019 Recanati, Italy

Lunar Design
537 Hamilton Avenue
Palo Alto, CA 94301

Machineart
66 Willow Avenue
Hoboken, NJ 07030

Vico Magistretti
c/o De Padova
Coreso Venezia 14
20121 Milan
Italy

Jovo Majstorovic
Art Center College of Design
1700 Lida Street
Pasadena, CA 91103

Matorell, Bohigas, MacKay
Diseño Ahorro Energetico SA (DAE)
c/o Leopoldo Mila/DAE
Poligono Industrial Sant Jordi S/n
08800 Vilanova I La Geltru
Barcelona, Spain

Larry McKinney
Industrial Design Department
California State Long Beach
3859 E. 8th Street
Long Beach, CA 90804

Jeff Meredith
Industrial Design Department
California State Long Beach
3859 E. 8th Street
Long Beach, CA 90804

Metaphase Design Group Inc.
1266 Andes Boulevard
St. Louis, MO 63132

Michael W Young Associates
45-28 11th St.
Long Island City, NY 11101

Leopoldo Mila
Poligono Industrial Sant Jordi S N
08800 Vilanova I La Geltru
Barcelona
Spain

Jørgen Møller
Danish Design Center
HC Andersens Boulevard 18
DK 1553 Copenhagen V
Denmark

Howard M. Montgomery
Cranbrook Academy of Art
1221 N. Woodward
Bloomfield Hills, MI 48304

Montgomery Design International
777 Oakmont Lane
Suite 600
Westmont, IL 60559

Montgomery Pfeiffer
Montgomery Pfeiffer Industrial Design
461 Bush Street
San Francisco, CA 94108

Dargen Moore
North Carolina State University
School of Design
Brooks Hall, Box 7701
Raleigh, NC 27695

Leslie Muller
Pratt Institute
396 Broome Street #16
New York, NY 10013

Kevin Byrd Murray
Western Washington University
Industrial Design Department
P.O. Box 5581
Bellingham, WA 98227

NCS Design Rio
Avenida Pasteur 405
Urva CEP 22290
Rio de Janeiro
Brazil

Neostudio Di R. Lanciani & W. Posern
c/o Luxo Italiana S.p.A.
Via Delle More 1
Presezzo, Bergamo
Italy

Alexander Neumeister
Neumeister Design
Von-Goebel-Platz 8
D-80638 Munich
Germany

Thomas J. Newhouse Designs
0-10923 2nd Avenue
Grand Rapids, MI 49504

Niels Diffrient Product Design
879 North Salem Road
Ridgefield, CT 06877

Ninaber/ Peters/Krouwel
Industrial Design
Noordeinde 2d
23111 CD Leiden
The Netherlands

Jean Nouvel
c/o Figueras International Seating
Ctra. De Pares A. Bigues
Spain

Now Product Design
955 Roble Ridge
Palo Alto, CA

Satyendra Pakhale
Meyboom Flat, Appt. 18
H.Gorterlaan - 2
5644 SW Eindhoven
The Netherlands

Palo Alto Design Group Inc.
360 University Avenue
Palo Alto, CA 94301

Ole Palsby
Danish Design Center
HC Andersens Boulevard 18
DK 1553 Copenhagen V
Denmark

Verner Panton
Kohlenberggasse 21
CH-4051 Basel
Switzerland

Pelikan Design
Danish Design Center
HC Andersens Boulevard 18
DK 1553 Copenhagen V
Denmark

Jorge Pensi
B. Lux S.A.
Poligono Eitua
S/No. 482401 Berriz
Vizcaya, Spain

Pentagram Design Ltd.
11 Neddham Road
London W11 2RP
England

Peter Stut Industrial Design
9761 Um Eelde,
The Netherlands

Montgomery Pfeifer
461 Bush Street
San Francisco, CA 94108

Olivetti Design Division
Via Porlezza 16
20123 Milan
Italy

Philippe Starck, Paris
Vitra GmbH
Charles Eames-Strasse 2
D-79576 Weil am Rhein
Germany

Philips Corporate Design
P.O. Box 218
5600 MD Eindhover
The Netherlands

Phoenix Product Design
Kolner Strasse 16
70376 Stuttgart
Germany

PI-Design AG
Kantonsstrasse
CH-6234 Triengen
Switzerland

Porsche Design GmbH
A-5700 Zell See
Flugplatzstrasse 29
Germany

Priority Designs
2803 Delmar Drive
Columbus, OH 43209

Product Insight Inc.
6 Ledgerock Way, Unit #1
Acton, MA 01720

Robert Rabinovitz
Cranbrook Academy of Art
1221 N. Woodward
Bloomfield Hills, MI 48304

River Studio
414 N. Mill Street
Aspen, CO 81611

RKS Design
7407 Topanga Cyn
Canoga Park, CA 91303

ROGOV International Design
6162 Nancy Ridge Drive
San Diego, CA 92121

Chris Root
North Carolina State University
School of Design
Brooks Hall, Box 7701
Raleigh, NC 27695

Troika Boll & Cie (Rubis S.A.)
Hattert
Germany

Ryan & Associates
110 S. Race #201
Urbana, IL 61801

Michael Schmick
The University of the Arts
Industrial Design Department
320 South Broad Street
Philadelphia, PA 19102

Stephan Schonherr
North Carolina State University
School of Design
Brooks Hall, Box 7701
Raleigh, NC 27695

Abigail Shachat
Cranbrook Academy of Art
1221 N. Woodward
Bloomfield Hills, MI 48304

Don Shepherd
Herman Miller Inc.
855 East Main Avenue
Zeeland, MI 49464

Anthony D. Shoemaker
204 1 2 S. Washington Street
New Bremen, OH 45869

Siemens Design
St.Martin-Strasse 76
D-81541, Munich, Germany

Smart Design Inc.
7 W. 18th Street
New York, NY 10011

Ettore Sottsass
Vitra GmbH
Charles Eames-Strasse 2
D-79576 Weil am Rhein, Germany

Splane Associates
10850 White Oak Avenue
Crenada Hills, CA 91344

Philippe Starck
Vitra GmbH
Charles Eames-Strasse 2
D-79576 Weil am Rhein, Germany

Steelcase Research &
Development/Industrial Design
Steelcase, Inc.
6100 East Paris, S.E.
Caledonia, MI 49316

Steiner Design Associates
& Synectic Engineering
214 Pemberwick Road
Greenwich, CT 06831

Mark Stockwell
Cranbrook Academy of Art
1221 N. Woodward
Bloomfield Hills, MI 48304

Studio Brown
6 Princes Buildings
Bath BA1 2ED, England

Bill Stumpf
William Stumpf Associates
128 N. 3rd Street
Minneapolis, MN 55401

Svein Asbornsen & Partners
c/o HÅG inc.
108 Landmark Drive
Greensboro, NC 27409

Marco Susani
Susani & Trimarchi Architects
Domus Academy
Strada 2 Edificio C-2
Milanofiori, 20090 Assago, Italy

Joe Tan
Art Center College of Design
1700 Lida Street
Pasadena, CA 91103

Tandem Industrial Design Group
10300 N. Tantan
Cupertino, CA 95016

Taylor & Chu
1831 Powell Street
San Francisco, CA 94133

Teague
14727 N.E. 87th Street
Redmond, WA 98052

Ilona Törmikoski
University of Art & Design Helsinki
Hameentie 135 C
00560 Helsinki, Finland

Tres Design Group Inc.
1440 N. Dayton Street
Chicago, IL 60622

Mario Trimarchi
Susani & Trimarchi Architects
Domus Academy
Strada 2 Edificio C-2
Milanofiori
20090 Assago
Italy

Trung Q Phung
Industrial Design Department
California State Long Beach
3859 E. 8th Street
Long Beach, CA 90804

TV & Video Systems Group,
Design Center
Sharp Corporation
Corporate Design Center
22-22 Nagaike-cho, Abeno-ku
Osaka 545, Japan

Petri Vainio
University of Art & Design Helsinki
Hameentie 135 C
00560 Helsinki, Finland

Vent Design
1436 White Oaks Road, Unit 15
Campbell, CA 95008

Via 4 Design GmbH
Inselstrasse 1
D-72202
Nagold, Germany

A. Viscasillas
Leopoldo Mila DAE
Poligono Industrial Sant Jordi S N
08800 Vilanova I La Geltru
Barcelona, Spain

Hannes Weibel
Art Center College of Design (Europe)
Château de Sully
Route de Chaily 144
Case Postale 32
1814 La Tour-de-Peilz
Switzerland

John C. Whiteman
Institute of Design
Illinois Institute of Technology
10 W. 35th Street
Chicago, IL 60614

Wiege
Wilkhahn
Entwicklungs GmbH
Haupstrasse 81
D-31848 Bad Münder
Germany

Woods & Brooks
11160 S.W. Highway
Paios Hills, IL 60465

WorkTools Inc./Innovations &
Development
20757 Plummer Street
Chatsworth, CA 91311

Worrell Design Inc.
6569 City West Parkway
Eden Prairie, MN 55344

Tony Wurman
The University of the Arts
Industrial Design Department
320 South Broad Street
Philadelphia, PA 19102

David Yim
Industrial Design Department
California State Long Beach
3859 E. 8th Street
Long Beach, CA 90804

Soren Yran
P. Yran & B. Storbraaten, Architects, Inc.
c/O HÅG inc.
108 Landmark Drive
Greensboro, NC 27409

Bruno Zacco
c/o Mercedes Benz
Munich
Germany

Ziba Design Inc.
305 N.W. 21st Avenue
Portland, OR 97209

David Zimberoff
Art Center College of Design
1700 Lida Street
Pasadena, CA 91103

Vladimir Zinovieff
Art Center College of Design (Europe)
Château de Sully
Route de Chaily 144
Case Postale 32
1814 La Tour-de-Peilz
Switzerland